THE FREE LANCE HUSTLE

THE COMPLETE GUIDE TO MAKING A LIVING AS A FREELANCE ARTIST

David Heredia

COPYRIGHT © 2019 BY DAVID HEREDIA. ALL RIGHTS RESERVED

The Freelance Hustle
Copyright © 2019 by David Heredia

ISBN (978-1-7344595-0-0)

TABLE OF CONTENTS

Chapter Five: Managing Clients

Chapter Six: Delivering Successful Proposals

Chapter Seven: Marketing techniques

Chapter Eight: How to Create Multiple Revenue Streams

Chapter Nine: You Must Believe it to Achieve it

Chapter Ten: Delivering a Successful Pitch

Chapter Eleven: Selling & Accomplishing Goals

Quick Guide
QR CODE SCANNER

Sprinkled throughout this book, you will see QR Codes like the one on the right which will grant you instant access to download files, and watch exclusive videos. Most cellphones already have a QR Code scanner installed. If not, you can download a free QR Code scanner app online. **Scan this code now.** You will get a pop-up message which will direct you to the **heroes of color website.** Try it now to make sure that it works! While you're there, enter your email and join our email list.

EXERCISES

This book is not intended for you to just read and then use it as a door stop. I want you to roll up your sleeves and get involved by doing all of the exercises and challenges in this book. Go at your own pace, but go. Your goals don't work unless you do.

ACKNOWLEDGEMENTS

First of all, I want to start by **THANKING YOU** for buying this book and supporting a fellow independent artist. We should all recognize that behind every successful person, there are hundreds of people who have impacted their lives. Every single freelance client that I have ever had, whether our experiences together were good, bad or awkward, has helped to shape me into the freelance entrepreneur that I have become.

MY FAMILY: To my lovely wife Sandra, thank you for putting up with all my crazy work hours – Te quiero mucho amor. To my Mother and all my brothers for complimenting my work at an early age and not shattering my confidence when it was evident that my work looked horrendous! Thank you, Carlos, for teaching me how to draw. Edwin, thank you for helping me to overcome and face my fears early on. Gerald Chertavian, your advice is the GPS system that I use to navigate my personal life and professional career. To all my family, thank you for believing in me when at times I didn't believe in myself.

COLLEGE OF THE CANYONS: To my indispensable business coaches of the Small Business Development Center - Catherine Grooms, Bandhana Katoch, Dr. Tora Brown, and Erica Bristol – thank you for all of your valuable advice. Your guidance has catapulted my business to another level. To Jeffrey Baker, Chair of the Media Entertainment Arts department, and Jeffrey Forrest, Vice President of the Economic and Workforce Development office: thank you both for supporting my vision, and for providing me with a platform to launch my "Business of Freelance" workshop series at the College. That workshop series is the foundation on which this book is built.

DAVID RHODES, PRESIDENT OF THE SCHOOL OF VISUAL ARTS: I want to thank you for your friendship and support for all of my business ventures. I also want to thank you for continuing to give me a platform to share my experiences with students early on in their careers.

MICHAEL HAGERMAN, MY SCRIPT EDITOR: Thank you for consistently turning my rough words into diamonds. You've helped make my "Heroes of Color" animated web series, become a seven-time award winning series. Thank you too for agreeing to edit this book!

EDUCATIONAL INSTITUTIONS: To all of the educational institutions that I have attended and credit with teaching me the skills to become the proverbial "jack of all trades" - The High School of Art & Design (Cartooning), New York City College of Technology (Advertising), The School of Visual Arts (Animation), Savanah College of Art & Design (Motion Graphics), College of the Canyons (3D Animation), and Glendale Community College (Motion Graphics) - thank you!

INTRODUCTION

"Impossible is just a big word thrown around by
small men who find it easier to live in the world they've
been given than to explore the power they have to
change it." -Muhammad Ali

Having your own business can be one of the most incredible experiences in your life. It allows you the flexibility to spend time with your family, earn money doing what you love, and make all the rules. In order to be a successful freelancer, you'll need skills that are not always taught to artists in college. Graduating with a BFA or an MFA does not automatically qualify you to run a freelancing business.

As the old saying goes, experience will be your best teacher, especially since experience gives you the test first and the lesson afterwards. You have to know who you are, what you have to offer, and if there is even a market for your products and services. This book will ask you to answer a number of questions, and require you to give some thought about the best direction you should take when searching for clients. My objective: to help you make more informed decisions while avoiding some of the mistakes that many freelancers tend to make early on in their business.

Freelancing has undoubtedly changed my life. Being a full-time freelancer has taken me on journeys that working for others would have never taken me. One of the many objectives of this book is to highlight not only the major triumphs of being a freelancer, but to also share some very important lessons learned. For example, I've learned not to use the word "failure," because you've only failed once you've given up.

Running a business is hard to do when all you want to do is draw or create. Be prepared to wear many different hats, and to answer to many different bosses; i.e., your clients. As a freelance entrepreneur, you will be forced to think about non-creative matters such as:

- How do I ensure that your clients are paying their invoices on time?
- How do I handle business tax returns?
- Do I need a lawyer here, and when?
- How do I legally protect my work via copyrights and trademarks?
- How do I price my work?
- Is healthcare affordable for the self-employed?

There is definitely a lot to consider when you become a freelancer, and we're just scratching the surface with that list. On a different level, overcoming self-doubt can be a constant struggle for creative people. We sabotage ourselves far more than any client ever could. While working for some major video game and animation studios, I continued to freelance on a part-time basis. In 2009, freelancing as a digital artist became my full-time job. It was the scariest decision of my life. Three years later, though, earning a six-figure income as a freelancer became a reality.

Lacking the business sense needed to maintain it, however, the six-figure income only lasted for three consecutive years. A complacent freelancer is a doomed freelancer! Yes, freelancing can be scary, unpredictable, but also it can be rewarding when you put your marketing strategies into action. A key point here: your success as a freelance entrepreneur will be determined by the opportunities you go out and create for yourself.

In this book, I am happy to share some very creative, actionable ideas that you can start putting into practice right now! With the gig economy on the rise, corporations and staffing agencies of all sizes are reducing their overhead expenses by hiring freelancers. Other companies such as Upwork have built an infrastructure entirely dedicated to serving freelance artists. So, if you want amazing insider tips on how to get a piece of this billion-dollar pie, this book is for you. Enough talk - let's get busy!

Chapter One

INTRO TO FREELANCING

IS THIS A BUSINESS OR A HOBBY?

Are you freelancing as a hobby or as a full-time job? How you answer that question will determine the trajectory that your freelance business will take. Sometimes we step into freelancing by mistake; other times it's by necessity. Unfortunately, perception can be powerful but it can also be misleading.

Let's say you meet someone in the elevator wearing a t-shirt and ripped jeans – maybe even a hat turned backwards. If this person tells you that they are a freelance artist, what would you think of them? Be honest. Now, take the same person in the elevator, but this time they are dressed in a business suit and tie. If this person tells you that they are a freelance entrepreneur, what would you think of them? Who commands more of your respect? Who would you think is more qualified for a job? Hopefully we are both thinking the same thing here.

Clearly our biases can get in the way of our reality. In my case, I have had to navigate the freelance world with a clear direction of where I want my career to take me. You have the ability to shape people's perception of you based on how you carry yourself, speak about yourself, and what freelance jobs you decide to take or turn down. I wanted people to treat me with the same respect you would give the freelancer who was wearing a suit versus the freelancer wearing a t-shirt and ripped jeans. They may both be equally qualified, but clients want to work with people that they deem trustworthy and responsible. In most situations, however, dressing up makes you look more professional.

You'll also need decide on how deeply you want to invest in this freelance game. Even if you freelance as a side hustle and keep your day job, this book will still be helpful to you. While your current day job may be driving you insane and you're just dying to quit, think twice about my story before making any emotional decisions. My introduction to freelancing was born out of necessity. In 1997, I was a junior in college at The New York City Technical College in Brooklyn, New York, and employed at the Academic Advisement Office registering incoming freshman. I was paid through a work-study program, but my work-study funds were about to end which meant that I would soon be out of a job and a paycheck. Worse yet, it was close to Christmas and suddenly I found myself desperately in need of money.

Faced with that reality, my idea was to let people know that I created custom cartoon designs. My problem: I didn't know how to ask for a sale. So, I started bringing in artwork and leaving it in places where I was sure people would see it. My co-workers took notice and soon everyone commented on how they all wanted a customized art piece. Once I landed my first client, I began offering custom designs to anyone who commented on my work.

My big break was when I volunteered to design the windows of our Advisement Office. I knew it had heavy foot traffic with faculty and students walking by it several times a day. I took my time and created three amazing Halloween designs. I designed a series of cute monsters using colored pencils and airbrush. One design of a purple witch seemed to get the most attention.

I then volunteered to design the windows for Christmas as well. The office secretary, Lucy Campisi Troia, invited faculty to come to the office and see the Christmas designs. It was an instant hit! Lucy introduced me to Francisco Betancourt, Chair of the Hospitality Management Department. He personally commissioned me to design two Christmas themed posters for his office and his home. He went on to introduce me to The Hale House Foundation as well as The Brooklyn Aids Task Force who both commissioned me for airbrushed pieces.

Commissioned piece hanging on wall in room dedication ceremony at the Brooklyn Aids Task Force in Brooklyn, NY 1997.

Sometimes customers don't realize what they want until they see what you have to offer. It's important to keep finding new ways to showcase your work. By putting my artwork in places that I knew had heavy traffic, I was able to get the attention of potential clients, who later became paying clients. I knew the people in the Advisement Office had to sit in a waiting room with nowhere else to look. Marketing genius that I didn't know I was, I had used my environment to my advantage.

The ability to ask for a sale is a skill I have learned and practiced through the years. I have found that through trial and error, even if you're not the most talented artist in the room, you can still create opportunities for yourself. But first, you need to know where you want to go with this freelancing business. Try this goal setting exercise:

PROS AND CONS OF FREELANCING

Whether you want to earn some cash on the side or make a living as a freelance designer, artist, etc., there are few things that you should consider before you run off and quit your day job. You need to make a key decision now: how much time do you want to invest in your freelance business? Do you want to do this on the side or do this full time? While there is no right or wrong answer, this will be a mindset that you need to prepare yourself for before starting the freelancing life.

Back in 2009, I had just been laid off from my job as a character designer with a video game company. My unemployment checks were about to run out, my first child was about to be born, and I had spent the better part of the year applying for full-time work with no success. I decided that with four months of unemployment checks remaining, I needed to make a choice. That led me to search for freelance work instead of a full-time job. It was a tremendous gamble and one of the first things I had to consider were the pros and cons. Your pros and cons list will look very different from mine, because our situations will be different. Still you must determine what advantages and disadvantages await you in the freelance world. Take a look at my actual list from 2009 on the next page:

PROS

- I can't get laid off
- I get to create my own hours, no time clocks to punch in
- I'm the boss and call the shots
- Flexibility to work from anywhere that has internet access.
- Limitless potential to earn money
- Creative companies & staffing agencies hire freelance designers
- I can create my own brand, message, and company objectives
- Independence
- I don't have to listen to or work near toxic people
- I can spend more time with the family
- If I get a full-time job, I can still do freelance work and earn extra cash on the side

CONS

- No job security or unemployment checks
- Unstable income and job opportunities
- I may have to work seven days a week to find freelance work
- I might get too comfortable working from home
- I don't have any co-workers to listen or speak to
- No health insurance or benefits
- No paid time off, sick leave, or vacation pay
- If I don't work, I don't get paid
- Bookkeeping and tax requirements

Looking back at this list, the pros slightly outweighed the cons. As a result, it wasn't a unanimous decision for me, and it still took some serious thought. The two big hurdles for me were taxes and the lack of benefits. Doing taxes for a small business was more difficult than I had anticipated. Retaining receipts, making P&L (profits and loss) reports, keeping track of mileage, etc. was a lot of work. I got it wrong a few times before I finally found a great tax person who walked me step-by-step through the process.

You have to be aware of a lot of other matters when starting your freelance business. My next big hurdle was benefits. When you are self-employed, you need some sort of medical coverage and let me tell you, "It isn't cheap." I lucked out because my wife had a great benefits package at her job, so I didn't have to worry about it later on in my career. Early on, however, I was paying close to $350 a month for medical and dental insurance.

There is so much more to consider, and it's difficult to know what the right steps to take are. Some of the best advice that I got early on was to speak to other freelancers, and ask how they are doing and what works for them. I asked several freelancers how they were doing financially. The general response: they were not doing well. It's both sad and frightening to hear that with so many freelance opportunities, so many freelancers haven't been able to really cash in. It's important, however, to find out exactly why they're doing so poorly. We can start by asking questions like:

- What's your marketing plan look like?
- Have you identified your target market?
- How do you know that this is your market?
- What are your short term and long-term goals?
- Where do you see yourself five years from now? 10 years?
- How are you marketing and promoting your services?
- Who is your ideal client and how are you connecting with them?
- Are you doing this full time or part time?
- Do you offer multiple services or just one?

Those are just some of the questions we should be asking, not just of other freelancers, but of ourselves. If you're comfortable enough, ask a freelancer if they are able to support themselves financially. If they are, ask them if you can become a part of their network, and build a relationship with them. Experience has proven that once you start to surround yourself with successful people, you start to learn their habits and you become more successful in meeting your objectives. I will get into building a strong support system in the next few chapters.

If, on the other hand, that freelancer isn't doing well, try to find out why. We learn from other people's mistakes too, so pay attention! I saw a great post on Instagram recently that had an image of a ferocious looking lion. The quote said "Don't follow your dreams, hunt them down!" As freelancers, we must develop an insatiable appetite for success. Granted, everyone has a different meaning of what success means, but the message is clear: you're not going to land gigs by simply stating that you are open for business. Instead you must consistently and constantly create opportunities for yourself.

EXERCISE #1 – THE PROS AND CONS OF FREELANCING

Jump on your laptop and create a pros and cons list for taking on some freelance work. Seriously think through what the advantages and disadvantages of freelancing might be for you. This list can help you decide how much time you want to invest in your freelancing business.

EIGHT ESSENTIAL QUALITIES OF A SUCCESSFUL FREELANCER

Where do you see yourself three years from now? Seriously, think about that. Have you planned that out? Well, it's not enough to just have a plan. If you don't put that plan into action, you will likely be in the exact same place you are in right now. It's often been said that if you're failing to plan, you're planning to fail. But the reality is, if you're failing to put your plans into action, you're destined to fail.

Here are eight essential qualities I believe that every successful freelancer should learn and develop as they grow their business:

- Business Savvy
- Self-Discipline
- Confidence
- Creating a Support System
- Finding your Passion
- Persistence
- Resourcefulness, and
- Versatility

Let me explain why these factors have been so critical to my success as a freelancer.

BECOME BUSINESS SAVVY

If you want to do business, then you need to learn some basic business practices. Typical examples include drafting artist's agreements, reading contracts, pricing your work, negotiating your rates, and protecting your intellectual property. Many other topics will be covered later in this book.

While attending The School of Visual Arts - New York City in 2000, I landed a freelance job with a small creative agency. I was hired to animate a Taco Bell commercial, and was supposed to be paid (I thought) $10,000 for 30 seconds of animation. Excited to get the assignment, I started the work without asking to see an agreement or contract. (Can you sense the trouble ahead?) When I finally took the time to read the contract,

I learned that "the creative agency would be paid $10,000" and not the "work for hire." I was the work for hire. By signing, I agreed to be paid $250 for my animation services.

This experience taught me several hard lessons. First and foremost, it illustrated (no pun intended) the importance of reading a contract before agreeing to it. If you don't understand the language, hire an entertainment attorney or other qualified lawyer to review it. If you don't have the money to hire an attorney, log onto score.org and find yourself a mentor who may be able to help decipher what you're reading for free. In California, you can go to www.calawyersforthearts.org, a non-profit organization dedicated to providing legal services to artists and members of the creative arts community. Bottom line: don't sign a contract that you don't understand! One of the reasons some artists get cheated or short-changed financially is because they treat their freelance business more like a hobby rather than a business.

YOU MUST BE SELF-DISCIPLINED

Being your own boss is one of my favorite parts of being an entrepreneur. But it requires a lot of self-discipline and old-fashioned hard work. One day in 2012, I was going to my first office space in Santa Clarita, California. I had a full agenda of client projects on my to-do list that day, and arrived around 8:30am. After I sat down, I read through my agenda and prepared to get to work.

Before I got started, I logged on to Netflix since I usually work while listening to cartoons in the background. I hardly ever watch the programs - it's just for ambience. Well, this time I didn't just listen to it, I watched almost an entire season worth of episodes of that particular show. Afterwards, I even took a two-hour lunch break! By 5:30pm, I had to go pick up my kids from childcare. As I left the office, I glanced at my to-do list and realized that I had made absolutely no progress that day. It was the least productive day of my life.

After I received some angry emails from clients requesting updates, I made sure that that day was the first and last time that I was unproductive in the office. Everyone needs to be disciplined, but this is even more critical when you are working for yourself. You must have self-discipline in order to meet your objectives. Planning just isn't enough. A well written to do list means nothing if you don't have the self-discipline to take action on that list. How many of us start a new design project and, midway through it, start another project? Most artists are guilty of that, including me. Your best bet: if you have a great idea, write it down and get back to it later. Get into the habit of finishing what you started.

BUILD AND MAINTAIN YOUR CONFIDENCE

You must believe in yourself and in your creative abilities. While we all have moments of self-doubt, dwelling on what you think you can't do or comparing your skills to others will hold you back before you even get started.

Consider another of my examples: Back in 2002, I remember wanting to attend the San Diego Comic Con as an exhibitor. Unfortunately, I had continuously sabotaged my chances of acceptance for years simply by saying that I couldn't do it because I wasn't good enough. In fact, I said it so much that I started to believe it.

In 2005, however, I decided to attend just so that I can speak to some of the exhibitors and learn what they did to prepare for the event. Everywhere I looked, I saw exhibitors who had incredible tables set up with posters, books, buttons, stickers, and cosplay characters posing near their tables. It was so entertaining that I felt like I was walking through a circus.

In this sea of exhibitor tables sat this quiet young man at a six-foot table decked out with amazing artwork and merchandise. He had no decorations, no free candy and no dazzling displays. In fact, his set up was so boring that it made you want to speed walk past his table. I was curious, so I stopped. As I began talking to him, I noticed that he only had one skinny comic book for sale. In the three days he had been there, he only sold five copies of his comic.

Somehow, though, the guy was really excited! He went on to explain how accomplished he felt. Accomplished? Did I miss something? With five comic book sales in a venue packed with thousands of people, I would have been depressed to say the least yet he felt a sense of accomplishment? After speaking with him, it was clear that he too was intimidated by exhibiting next to hundreds of his competitors. Still, he believed in himself enough to do it. He was a success because he overcame his fear of exhibiting at Comic Con.

I bought a copy of his comic book, and thanked him for giving me the inspiration I needed to apply the following year. For the next five years, I too exhibited at the San Diego Comic Con thanks to this young man. Bottom line: one important way to start building your confidence is to eliminate the word "can't" from your vocabulary. As I always tell my students, "Convince yourself, not your clients." At the end of the day, if you don't believe in yourself, no one else will either.

At my both in San Diego Comic Con 2006.

CREATE A SUPPORT SYSTEM

Pay attention - this is a big one! Every entrepreneur needs a support system. Surround yourself with people who empower you, challenge you and force you to "level up." If you have any toxic people in your circle, you must remove yourself from them immediately. They might be people you know very well. They might be close friends or even family.

Try not to take it personally. It may not have anything to do with you. Toxic people tend to project their own fears on to you. They may simply be too afraid to take the big risks that you are willing to take. Here are a few of the most toxic people that you might recognize:

- **Energy Vampires:** You've met them - they're the ones who suck the positivity and joy out of everything you do. No matter how great your good news is, they'll only find the negative in it.
- **The Haters:** They watch everything you do closely. They may wish you well to your face, but they secretly hope you fail. They are incredibly deceiving because they could be your close friends. They typically project their own fears on to you by telling you that you can't do something that they do not have the courage to do.
- **The Leeches:** These are people who talk big but, for whatever reason, rarely if ever actually accomplish their own goals. They are opportunists, and may seem to jump around from person to person in the hopes of leeching off of the success of others.
- **The Dream Crusher:** There is no stopping the dream crusher! They can run over your dreams, goals and aspirations like a Sherman tank. They may even try to make you feel bad for daring to be successful.
- **The Narcissist:** No matter what you've accomplished, it's never good enough for them. They love to take center stage and specialize in turning the conversation back to themselves. They are constantly looking for ways to "out do" your achievement by mentioning an achievement of their own, even if it was two decades ago.

Throughout this book, you will hear me talk about my Business of Freelancing workshops. In one of my recent workshops conducted at College of the Canyons in Santa Clarita, I witnessed the true meaning of what it means to support someone. There was a couple, Shari and Kevin, who had signed up for the workshop and attended the first day of the three-day course.

Kevin is a photographer and videographer with a fulltime job. Since my classes were held on Friday mornings, he was only able to take one day off from his job to attend the workshop. Shari attended all three days. As we were all saying our goodbyes on the last day of the workshop, Shari was handing out business cards. But when I looked at them, they were Kevin's business cards, not hers.

I found out that Shari is a registered nurse and is not even a freelancer! So, what was she doing there? Well, since Kevin wasn't able to attend the workshops that he valued so much, Shari was able to take the time off to attend the classes, learn the materials, and pass the lessons on to Kevin. I was not expecting that. What a beautiful demonstration of love and support.

Count yourself lucky if you have someone like this in your life. Sometimes just being around supportive people can give you the confidence you need to close your next deal. Having confidence in yourself is an essential quality you need when pitching proposals to your clients.

Business of Freelance workshop – March 2019.

FINDING YOUR PASSION - IDENTIFY YOUR GIFT

It's often been said that if you choose a job that you love, you'll never work a day in your life. The idea is pretty clear: when you are getting paid to do something that you enjoy, it hardly feels like work. We all have a gift, but you have to identify it.

I hate to sound cliché, but if you were told that you could land any creative job in the world, what position would you apply for? Your answer to that question might be the first clue as to the type of work you are passionate about doing. When you find a job that feeds your passion, you will thrive at it. Since most of us spend the majority of our weekdays working, we might as well get paid to do something we enjoy.

PERSISTENCE

Freelancing will present you with challenges that can make or break you. In 2015, I created an educational animated series called "Heroes of Color." It was well received by the public, and went on to win six film festival awards ranging from best short story to best animation. In 2016, I developed a children's book idea based on "Heroes of Color," and pitched it to Scholastic, a major children's book publisher that, among other titles, has published the Harry Potter series.

The idea was rejected exactly 11 minutes after I sent the email out. I submitted several more ideas throughout that year, but none of them seemed to raise so much as an eyebrow. Some people told me that my books were being rejected because I didn't have an agent. Others said my idea wasn't unique enough. Despite everyone's speculation, I believed in my product and I never gave up on submitting my ideas.

In 2018, my "Heroes of Color" series was written up in the New York Times, and I was invited to give a lecture and screening at the Schomburg Center in Harlem. In the audience was Channel 11 News. Before I knew it, I was on the local nightly news. When I got back to Los Angeles, I was contacted by my local National Public Radio (NPR) station. The producers actually came to my home for an interview about "Heroes of Color."

Now I was armed with some serious publicity. My mentor, Gerald Chertavian, suggested that I reach out to Scholastic again. In March of

2018, I once again emailed Scholastic to pitch the original "Heroes of Color" children's book idea that Scholastic had rejected in 2016. This time, my pitch resulted in a major book publishing deal!

Original book mock-ups submitted to Scholastic in 2016.

Why was it picked up this time? Was it good timing? Maybe. Good luck? Perhaps. But one thing I know for sure: if I had simply given up and stopped presenting my children's book ideas to Scholastic, I would have never landed the book deal. "Persistence overcomes resistance," is one of my favorite inspirational quotes that serves as a reminder that you must not give up on yourself, your dreams, or your goals.

RESOURCEFULNESS

Tap into the resources that are around you. Find answers online, watch lots of tutorials, ask for advice, enroll in a class or workshop, get a business coach or mentor, and never stop learning. When I landed a major animation project with Pearson Education in 2011, I went from working from home to working in an office with multiple freelancers working for me. I knew that I would not be able to manage this on my own, so I signed up to get a business coach via the Small Business Development Center (SBDC) at the local community college. It's a free resource that has enabled my business to grow in directions that I had never thought of. You don't need to have all of the answers, but try to surround yourself with people who do.

VERSATILITY

It's no secret: diversifying your creative services makes you more appealing than the freelancer who can just offer one service. This gives you the ability to "upsell" or add on additional items to your original sale. For example, I had a client that wanted a logo design. As we went over the details of his design, he asked if I knew anyone who did animated explainer videos. The answer: I graduated from school with an animation degree! I immediately sent him to my website, and provided my animation rates on the spot. Instead of closing him on one creative project, I was able to close the deal on multiple design services.

Some may disagree with the concept of being "A jack of all trades, and a master of none." That is, you do a lot of different things well, but are not exceptional at one specific thing. Since my revenue was dependent on my ability to close deals, I needed to offer as many different products as possible in order to make myself more marketable to clients.

Diversifying my design services has enabled me to tackle many different styles and a wide range of projects. Some of those projects include self-publishing a coloring book, stickers, animation, graphic design and even editing for a music.

Chapter Two

BRAND DEVELOPMENT

"It takes 20 years to build a reputation and five minutes to ruin it. If you think about that, you'll do things differently."
- Warren Buffett

HOW DO YOU DEFINE YOUR BRAND?

Your brand is the personality of your business. Two companies can sell the same products, but their brands could be total opposites. One brand though might entice a customer more just based on its core values or its activism towards current issues in society. What emotions do you want people to feel when they think of your company? It's up to you to shape and mold the feelings you want people to have when they think of your company based on the core values of your company. These core values are the foundation of what your company stands for. If the design job you are offered requires you to violate your principles, you might want to reconsider taking that project on.

That happened to me in 2008. I was offered an amazing freelance opportunity to become a comic strip illustrator for one of the leading Hip-Hop magazines in the US at that time. I was offered $500 to create a four-panel comic strip. When the director sent me the script, my jaw dropped to the floor!

The script was loaded with bad language from start to finish. This challenged my core values, and put me in a bad position because I really needed the money. I read the script roughly five times just to make sure that I hadn't misread it. Yup, all of that terrible language was still there. I called my brothers for advice. One of them suggested that I take the project, but not sign my name. This way nobody would know that I did it. He was right, but the problem was that I would know that I did it. At the end of the day, it was my ethics that were being tested, not my brothers'.

Reluctantly, I called the Art Director back to express my disapproval of the script. My comment: **"I know this is going sound real corny, but I don't want to promote this type of language in any of the work that I do."** The director went on to express that this was the style of writing that the editor wanted for the strip because he wanted it to be "edgy." I responded, **"You can be edgy without cursing. You just need good writing."**

The phone went silent. In my mind, I knew I blew it. I went on to explain, "Unless the editor is willing to remove all of the bad language, I am afraid I just can't take this project on. It goes against all of my principles as an artist. There is already enough bad language out there, so I don't want to contribute to it." There was continued total silence on the other end of the call.

Talk about an awkward moment. I hung up the phone and assumed that was the end of the project. When it hit me that I just turned down the easiest paycheck in my history as a freelance artist, I was upset with myself. Just as I started to punish myself for sticking to my morals, the phone rang. It was the Art Director. **"Yo Dave,"** he called out. **"I spoke to the editor and we both respect you for the decision that you made. Because of that, he is willing to remove all of the bad language of the script!"** It was the first time (and wouldn't be the last time) that I risked losing everything because I didn't want my brand associated with the clients' creative vision. Moral of that story: Protect your company's reputation, stay true to your core values. People will respect you for it.

Rough comic strip designed for Vibe Magazine.

Revised comic strip used in Vibe Magazine.

THE LOGLINE

In television and the movies, screenwriters are tasked with the incredibly difficult job of summing up their television show or movie in one sentence which is usually called a logline. In the business world, a logline helps you structure your "elevator pitch." The idea is that you want to give a clear, concise and engaging answer when someone asks you "What do you do?"

The logline identifies the key elements of your business and what you can do for that person. It should be short, catchy, easy to say, and even easier to remember. When creating your logline, try to include one thing that you want your audience to remember about your products, services or business.

Imagine this: there are two watches on the table. One is $5 and the other is $500. They both tell the time the same way. The more expensive watch, however, might be marketed as "The successful entrepreneur's watch." This logline leads the consumer to believe that if they buy this $500 watch, they are buying into the notion that they are a successful entrepreneur. Sell people on the benefits of your products or on the problems your products will solve for them.

Recently, I met a new business owner in the office building where I rent space. As we walked alongside each other, I asked what she did and she said, "I sell home insurance." My thought was that her attempt at a logline was boring and unengaging, and I did not want to ask her any more questions about her business.

Then, she asked me, "What do you?" I responded, "Have you ever heard of the term starving artists?" She replied, "yea." I continued: "Well, I teach them how to feed themselves through professional development workshops." She smiled, laughed and then started with a barrage of questions. I could have said, "I teach workshops at the local college," but the conversation might have ended there.

If you paint, you're not just a painter. Instead "you give birth to life through acrylics." Getting a potential customer's attention isn't enough. Jazz it up, because you only have a few seconds to keep their attention. Look for ways to prompt further conversations about what you do and what you can do for that potential client. Create loglines that get people excited.

PROTECTING YOUR BRAND

Now that you've taken great pains to develop your brand, how do you protect it? Refusing questionable freelance projects is one way to protect your brand, but it's not enough. While your character truly defines "who" you are, your reputation is merely what people "think" you are. Before a client decides if they want to reach out to you, they might Google you, check your website, or check your activity on social media.

Your reputation can help you close a sale or lose a sale before you even speak to a client. Even though you don't have the power to control what people think about you or your company, you can use the power of perception as leverage in crafting the story of what your company is all about. Use social media sites as tools to help build your reputation. Be careful though: social media can be a double-edged sword since it can also rip your reputation to shreds.

Let your uplifting photos and videos on social media speak for you. Getting into the habit of posting positive content can help influence potential clients to want to work with you. Those positive posts often help you obtain clients and get jobs as well! One of the first places job recruiters research after receiving an impressive resume is social media.

It's a 21st Century contradiction: people tend to lie on their resumes, but oddly reveal themselves through social media. We are constantly being judged, and social media is just another way for people to judge you. So, use it to your advantage.

Recently I posted a job for a temporary office assistant. I settled on a strong candidate, and we spoke on the telephone. He definitely said all the right things. Before I scheduled our first interview, I wanted to dig a little deeper so I looked him up on social media. I was shocked to see how disrespectful he was towards women and people of color. That led me to check other social media pages - perhaps I had the wrong person. No mistake, it was him. Needless to say, there was no follow-on interview.

It's a sad fact that we often sabotage our own success. Don't let your social media presence ruin your reputation. Instead use it to uplift you and your company since your next client might be swayed by your social media content. Constantly review your social media pages. Critically consider the content that you have posted. Now ask yourself, would you hire yourself after seeing all these posts?

CREATE YOUR IDENTITY

Once you have established your company's core values or mission statement, think about the identity of your company. What does your logo look like? What colors will you use? Do you have a tagline? These are all things that help define your company's identity, but I never gave "identity" much thought early on in my freelancing career.

I have always considered myself a cartoonist, so when I took on freelance projects, my main objectives were to get cartoon-related freelance gigs. My logo, however, was very boring, literally a black and white and somewhat corporate looking thing. My other issue: the logo didn't tell people the type of creative services that I offered. With an oval black and white logo that said "Heredia Designs," I was not surprised at the number of corporate branding gigs that I landed.

Once I realized this, I tilted the logo, periodically changed the colors, and began associating it with a cartoon character. It looked so much more fun. People got used to seeing my logo with a cartoon character beside it, and suddenly the cartoon gigs started coming my way. Since your logo is the face of your company, put some time into creating one that tells people exactly what you want them to know about you, your company, and the creative services that you offer.

EXERCISE #3 - CREATE YOUR IDENTITY PACKET

Don't think of yourself as an individual - you are now a company. Answer the following questions and let's define your company in further detail.

- What is your company name?
- Outline a detailed list of design or other creative services that you can offer.
- Who is your intended target market? How will you reach them?
- Design a rough logo that reflects the type of services you will offer.
- How will you operate your business? A sole proprietorship or an LLC (Limited Liability Company)?
- Have you checked to see if your company name is available for use?
- Have you checked to see if a URL exists with your desired company name?
- What makes your services unique to similar creative services?

IDENTIFY YOUR TARGET MARKET

Your target market can help you define your company's identity. If, for example, you want to attract surfers, your identity packet should contain images that surfers associate with surfing. As you begin developing your business, you will have to think about how you will actually reach your target market.

Who do you create your work for? Children, adults, comic book fans, or other groups? Identifying your target market is important, but knowing how to reach them is especially critical to your success. If you don't know who you're targeting or what their needs are, you can't expect anyone to bite. Once you've identified your clients' needs, you can create products specifically designed to grab their attention. Once you know what your ideal client wants, however, you need to figure out where to find them.

Here's a great tip: Reach out to your best (or most ideal client) and ask them what social media platforms they frequent and why. How frequently do they use those platforms, and what gets their attention the most online? Understand your clients' habits so that you can position yourself to be directly in their social media line of fire.

Sometimes you can totally misread your intended target market, but end up grabbing a different demographic. In 2008 I created a multicultural art print series intended specifically for junior high school students. It was a way for them to take pride in their cultures. I had researched and interviewed junior high schoolers to measure their levels of interest in my series.

While many of them liked the concept and the artwork, I found that people 20 years old and over (mostly college students, educators and people of color) connected with the art series even more than the junior high school students. So, even though I intended to hit one target market, I actually (and happily!) ended up reaching a broader target market by mistake.

If this new "accidental" target market falls in line with your company objectives, then go for it. If, however, that accidental market compromises your ethics even a little bit, don't take the gig. Stay true to your brand and the core values of your company. You don't have to accept every freelance job that comes your way, especially if that job compromises your brand and core values.

Remember that you're in the business of solving problems, not pleasing everyone. Your mission statement defines the core values of your company. This is your "why." Why are you doing what you are doing? What inspired you, motivated you, and what positive impact do you hope to achieve? Still, certain opportunities might not fall in line with your company objectives. If the gig doesn't feel right, don't take it.

Your ethics are the GPS of your company. That GPS warns you when you're about to take a wrong turn. Throughout your career, your ethics will be tested. In 2001, I almost took a spectacularly wrong turn.

A potential client had reached out to me because he wanted to hire me for a freelance job. It started off innocently enough. He did his research and opened our discussion with compliments on my work. **(Tip #1: Sincere compliments always get people's attention.)**

The client began to connect the dots and talk about all the schools, interests and friends we had in common. **(Tip #2: Finding common ground builds trust. Do your research on a potential client so that you can make quicker connections.)** Now that he had my undivided attention, he made his pitch. "I want to hire your animation studio to create a 60-minute animated film." The details of the proposed job:

- **The Hook:** They offered me $200,000.
- **The Catch:** It was animated pornography.
- **My Dilemma:** I needed the money, but it went against every moral fiber in my body.
- **The Outcome:** I always knew that I wanted to educate through art. Accepting this job would not have been a step in that direction. As much as I needed the money, I had to decline. This assignment definitely would have ruined my career.

When you are secure in the reasons you are doing business, it will become easier to turn down opportunities that you think will stain or even ruin your career. Spend time building and protecting your reputation. There is not enough money in the world worth compromising your ethics over. I have said it before, and I'll say it again: your ethics are the GPS of your company that will warn you when you're about to take a wrong turn. Listen to that GPS!

HEROES OF COLOR, LLC © COPYRIGHT 2019

CONNECTING THE DOTS

Do you remember that "connecting the dots" game we used to create images as children? We were given all the dots we needed to complete the picture. As we began connecting the dots, we moved from one dot to the next one very slowly because we didn't have a clear vision of what the big picture would look like. Once the image started to reveal itself, we gained more confidence. Networking is very much like connecting the dots.

Each of us has a unique set of dots – people - in our lives that we need to align in order to help us reveal our vision or the "big picture." Sometimes we have to be a bit aggressive about connecting these "dots." Going to professional social mixers and industry-related events can be very helpful. If you need to network with the director of the arts commission in your city, then you need to make sure you attend the city functions that that director attends. If the director is not there, speak to someone on the local arts commission, and ask for an introduction to the director. Connections are of course easier to make when you come recommended by a close colleague or friend of your potential new connection.

As an entrepreneur, you will learn how to turn introductions into opportunities, though it may require you to politely and persistently follow up. Some connections are made quickly while others can take years to forge. Sometimes, though, you will end up making casual connections in the most unlikely places that can lead to major payoffs.

STRATEGIC NETWORKING

Networking isn't just about meeting new people. It's about making deliberate connections with people that you feel can help move your business forward. In 2016, I wanted to develop a series of freelance workshops for college students. My target was animation majors at my local community college, the College of The Canyons in Santa Clarita, California. In order to get to the animation majors, I knew that I needed to meet with Jeffrey Baker, the head of the animation department. He was however incredibly busy and extremely hard to reach.

Confident that he would love my workshop idea, I had to find another way to reach him. So, I kept digging and found out that he actually taught a few 3D Animation courses. Solution: I signed up for one of his animation classes. Once I began attending his class, I began striking up conversations with him. It took me an entire semester to develop this relationship, and it was great to see that we had a lot in common. I learned that he used to freelance before he became a teacher and that was the hook I needed. Once I found a common ground, I pitched my freelance workshop idea.

He loved the idea, but we had to work on ways to get the workshop funded by the college. Three years later, I was contracted to teach my first "Business of Freelance" workshop at College of The Canyons. Since my conventional plan to reach the head of the animation department didn't work, I had to create a non-conventional path to reach him. Networking is important, but networking with a purpose can really help you connect your dots a lot faster.

Truck I created in the 3D Animation class.

ACCIDENTAL NETWORKING

In 2011, I was hired to create a cartoon movie poster for a client named Danny Hastings. He just penned a licensing deal for his live action comedy film called "The Love Potion" to the bilingual Viacom-owned cable network called MTV Tres. At the time, this was one of the most watched cable channels in the U.S. since the network targeted Latin millennials using brightly colored pop shows, music videos, movies and original programming. After making this connection, I immediately started to think that my multicultural art series could be a great fit with MTV Tres. Clearly, I needed to meet the person who offered Danny his licensing deal.

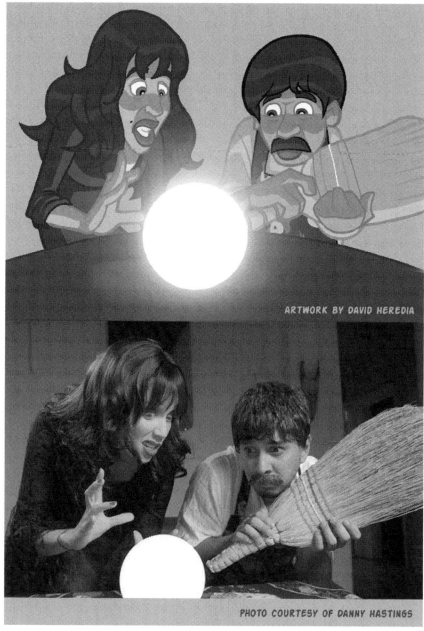

Reference photo used to create designs for movie poster.

Well, I got my opportunity in a pretty embarrassing way. Danny held a screening of his movie in New York City in February 2012, and invited everyone to attend. It was an amazing screening and after the movie ended, Danny took some questions from the audience. Some audience members commented on how great the artwork was for the movie poster, and even asked if there were talks to create an animated "Love Potion" film using the characters.

Danny responded, "You'd have to ask Chrystin Nevarez. She is the one responsible for offering me the licensing deal at MTV Tres." Bingo, now I had a name! Everything else that happened that evening was a blur. Needless to say, I kept my eyes focused on Chrystin for the rest of the night. As soon as the Q&A ended, I rushed toward her as she headed for the elevator. I wanted to introduce myself and use the opportunity to speak to her about my multicultural project.

My heart sank when I saw the elevator doors open, and Chrystin casually walked in with the rest of the crowd. Just as the doors began to close, I took a huge leap, knocking about five people to the ground, and shoved my arm into the closing doors. Nothing happened for about 5 seconds. I can imagine how funny it must have looked from inside the elevator seeing a part of an arm just sort of floating in between the doors. I could hear some laughter which grew louder as the door finally opened.

Everyone stared back at me while I stared at Chrystin, and I wasted no time in introducing myself as the designer of the movie poster. (This was my first elevator pitch in an actual elevator!) There was no room for me to get in, so I had to make it brief. I asked her for her business card but she quickly replied, "I don't have one." Just as the doors began to close again, I handed her my very cartoony business card. She took it, the door closed and that's where it would've ended until Danny's misfortune opened the door to my opportunity.

Danny was scheduled for a pitch meeting with Chrystin at MTV that same week. He wanted to pitch a few show ideas, and asked me if I was interested in attending. I was scheduled to fly back to L.A. the next day, but couldn't refuse the offer. Instead I changed my flight so that I can stay a few extra days. New York City traffic being what it is, I made sure that on that day I arrived at MTV 15 minutes early.

Suddenly my cellphone rang. At the other end of the line was a panicked Danny. He asked me to go up to Chrystin's office and keep her busy until he arrived. He was stuck in traffic and wouldn't arrive for another 45 minutes! He added that Chrystin was expecting me. Somewhat in disbelief at my big chance, I made my way up to her floor. As I walked into her office, the very first thing that I saw was my cartoony business card stuck upright in between the rows of her computer keyboard!

Not sure what to say at this point, I made a joke that if an NBA recruiter had witnessed my leap over the crowd that night, I would have been sitting at the NBA corporate office instead of hers. As we laughed, the ice was broken and we began talking. Danny never showed up. I spent 60 minutes in Chrystin's office, and we developed an amazing friendship that has lasted ever since.

Chrystin gave me some incredible industry advice on pitching animated projects, creating proposals and even some valuable insider information. Two years later, I presented a licensing proposal to MTV Tres for an animated multicultural show which Chrystin herself green lighted! Unfortunately, the show never saw the light of day due to layoffs that plagued the company that year. Still, it was an accidental networking opportunity that developed into something bigger because I continued to put myself in the right place at the right time.

MAKING CASUAL CONNECTIONS

When you have a goal in mind, you increase your chances of forging unlikely relationships that can help you get closer to accomplishing your objectives. For example, I forged an unlikely relationship with the CEO of a major, globally-recognized organization which ultimately led to me landing a publishing deal at Scholastic Corporation. Here's how it went down.

In 2016, my mentor, Gerald Chertavian, invited me to attend a business summit in Los Angeles. Gerald was asked to present awards to three of the nations' most influential business leaders. Prior to the presentation, the event offered some incredible ice breaker workshops which were RSVP only. Unfortunately, when I went to sign up, I was told that I was not an invited guest and could not attend any of the workshops.

There was an interesting poetry writing workshop that I really wanted to attend. I sat back and observed as people signed in, and noticed how distracted the host was when people stopped to ask questions. I waited for the perfect moment to slip in. As the host stopped to redirect some people off to a different workshop, I casually walked right in and took a seat.

The instructor who led the workshop was an award-winning poet named In-Q. He first read some poetry to us. Next he asked us to write a poem where we imagined that we were currently living the life that we always wanted. Amazingly this was the perfect platform I needed to test my elevator pitch to a room full of business professionals! In fact, I had been looking for new ways to promote my educational, animated series "Heroes of Color." This was definitely the moment I had been waiting for.

In-Q asked for a volunteer to read their poem. I jumped at the chance to be first even though I had no clue who my audience was, what their values were, or what industries they were in. I told a very personal story of how I turned my adversity into an opportunity. In part I spoke about how I was discriminated against in Los Angeles for being an Afro-Latino, and how those events drove me to promote cultural education through animation.

After the workshop ended, I spoke with the instructor and two other workshop attendees. One of them was Deborah Dugan, the former CEO of RED, the AIDS organization founded by Bono and Bobby Shriver to engage the world's most iconic brands in the AIDS fight. As we walked and talked, we learned more about each other and exchanged business cards. She loved the designs and cartoon illustrations of my "Heroes of Color" business card. She also wondered if I had a children's book in progress.

I didn't have a book planned at that point but, recognizing that a potential opportunity was approaching, I said that I did. That prompted her to give me the contact information for her friend, Andrea Pinkney, a vice president at Scholastic Corporation. Two years later, after that long journey from the poetry workshop, I landed a book publishing deal with Scholastic.

To me, there is no such thing as just a casual conversation. Instead, for an entrepreneur, your latest conversation is just another opportunity to share your passion with someone else. When that person shares your passion, powerful things can happen. Needless to say, you have to take advantage of every opportunity you can to get such conversations. If you don't get invited to social mixers and events, then find one online and attend it. When you know exactly what you want, it becomes a lot easier to obtain it.

NETWORKING LEADS TO PAID GIGS

One of the things I recently discovered about the power of networking is that it can also lead to paid freelance opportunities. Actively share your vision with others whenever you get a chance because you just don't know who they might know. Part of my company's mission is to offer creative development workshops. Recently I created an art program for kids aged 8-15 years old. The program is called "Junior Artrepreneurs." The objective of the program is to help turn young artists into entrepreneurs. The eight-week class went incredibly well and exceeded my expectations.

I ran the program, September 2019 at the local church. One of my goals was to expand the program and build support from local educational leaders in my community of Santa Clarita, California. One of our local professionals, Dr. Cherise Moore, is on the board of the Hart School District in the city of Santa Clarita. I reached out to her and slowly we began building the program locally.

Five months after the success of my junior arts class, I mentioned to Dr. Moore that I wanted to start offering day-long workshops to introduce the program to different schools. She was also on the Board of Jack & Jill of America which had a local chapter in my town. Now that she was aware of my vision, she spoke highly of me to the rest of the Board members of the Jack & Jill organization. Shortly after this, Jack & Jill hired me for a day-long workshop, where students created their own custom trucker hats.

You need to speak your goals into existence. Make people aware of your objectives because you never know who is in their network. Bottom line: the ability to turn introductions into opportunities is what entrepreneurship is all about.

Posing with students after custom hat workshop ended.

EXERCISE #4 - STRENGTHEN YOUR NETWORK

Pick a social network that most of your prospective clients use. Contact all of the followers in your list that meet your criteria of an ideal client. Send an individual direct message to each one of them. Tell them that you are building your email list and would love to add them to it. If you want to control who views your content, collect their emails and contact them yourself.

NETWORKING TIPS

It's important to realize that we can't do everything alone. For that reason, creating a support system is crucial. Although freelancing offers incredible independence, it doesn't mean that we have to do it all alone. One idea is to attend an industry related event where you will have more things in common with the attendees. Realistically some people have a hard time networking at social mixers, and striking up conversations with sometimes half-drunk people they don't know. I still struggle at those types of events, but have learned a few things to help ease me through those dreadfully awkward moments. Here are nine quick tips to consider:

- **Find Commonalities:** Are you into animation? Comic books? Photography? Where did you go to school? Any common ground that you can discover is bound to open a new door with your contact.
- Been there, done that: If you want to go somewhere with your career, it's great to speak with someone who has already been there. Spend time with like-minded individuals or seek them out at industry events such as conventions.
- **Join the club:** There are dozens of free clubs you can join both online and in person. You can use them as a way to bounce ideas off of other members, get advice, and learn new tips.
- **Social Media:** Probably the most obvious and easiest form of "free" networking is social media. Get into the habit of leaving comments, reposting, sharing and promoting other people's projects. The more you engage, the stronger your relationship will be with that individual.
- **It's not all about you:** Actually, it's about getting to know them. Ask, listen and observe. People love talking to a good listener.
- **Save the Elevator Pitch for the elevator:** Your mission in networking is to focus on making a connection, not a sales pitch.

Just chill out and have fun with it. The sales pitch will follow once you've solidified a connection.

- **Offer to help:** Always offer to help others with something before you ask them for help.
- **Follow Up:** This is a major one! So many of my successes have come from the follow up emails, calls and text messages that I have sent after meeting someone. Always follow up!
- **B.Y.O.F:** Bring your own friend to a social mixer or event. This can help you feel more comfortable and fill you with more confidence as you network.

CHOOSING THE RIGHT SOCIAL MEDIA NETWORK

Social Media has changed the way we communicate and reach people. It's an amazing tool to build your network. It allows us the opportunity to reach people who we normally would not have access to. Equally as important is knowing which social media platform to use in order to reach your target market.

In the summer of 2019, I set out to build relationships with community colleges and introduce them to my freelance workshop. Since I would be reaching out to professionals in higher education, I knew Instagram and Facebook were not my best options. In an effort to reach college professionals, it made more sense to focus my efforts on professional networks.

Knowing where to locate your target market is key. This way you can ensure that you are getting your products and services in front of the right people. One of the best ways to strengthen your relationships with your contacts online is to actively engage with them. Engage them by leaving comments and sending direct messages. People are more likely to take interest in you when you show an interest in what they are doing.

Don't be fooled in thinking that you need to have a lot of followers to have a strong network. Knowing the right people is better than knowing a lot of people you never actually engage with. While I understand perception is very important online, you have to know that your online statistics can be easily verified. One quick way to get an idea of how strong of an online following you have is review the number of engagements you get (likes, comments, etc.) in comparison to your followers. Frankly I get really suspicious of accounts of people who have 1 million followers, but are only getting 100 likes or comments on their posts.

Your objective on social media should be to build your own personal list. As you gain new followers and fans, start asking them for their email addresses to start building your email list. Think about it this way: if all social media sites crashed tomorrow, how many of your followers will you still be able to get in touch with?

Start bringing your followers into your world, so that you can create a more meaningful relationship with them. Sometimes when you reach out and attempt to make a new contact, the responses can be slow or you may not get any responses at all. If it's an important connection that you are trying to make, you have to be persistent. I'll give you another example.

Some time ago, I was trying to make a very important connection with Carl McNair on Facebook. I had just finished working on a "Heroes of Color" video episode honoring the accomplishments of his late brother, NASA Astronaut Dr. Ronald McNair. I started by reaching out to Carl on Facebook by sending him a direct message. My intent was to show him the video and get his approval. After two weeks of no response, I searched his page and saw that he was very active on Facebook. I needed to think of a new plan to get his attention.

This led me to go through every single post he had recently made, hit the "like" button, and leave comments on all of them. The next day, Carl finally responded to my direct email! Since then, we've been able to build a great relationship by having several phone conversations. Best of all, I now have gained his full support for the "Heroes of Color" video about his brother.

LET'S CONNECT RIGHT NOW
Let's network online right now. Scan this QR Code and let's build on Instagram today.

Chapter Four
CONTRACTS AND NEGOTIATIONS

IT'S OK TO SAY NO!

A basic concept here: you do not have to accept every single freelance project that a client wants to commission you for. As a freelancer, of course, we rarely turn projects down. Even with a full plate, we still try to find ways to squeeze in another project. When I first started freelancing, I never turned a client away. Quickly though I found that that was a rookie mistake.

Some clients were so incredibly difficult to work with that I regretted my decision to take them on at all. Difficult clients usually raise red flags right from the beginning but, because we are anxious to take on a client, we may ignore the signs. Pay attention to those red flags! Even if the client isn't difficult to work with, but you get an uneasy feeling about it, ask your mentor for advice before agreeing to take a project on from that client.

In 2000, as a second-year animation student at The School of Visual Arts in New York, I worked on an internship at Autonomy Media in Los Angeles. At Autonomy Media, I worked on some amazing projects including creating animated Gifs and motion graphics for websites. During my break, I would work on pencil tests which are rough animated sequences that are done in pencil.

The CEO of the company brought one of his friends to the office, and introduced himself to everyone only as Josh. Josh walked by my desk and saw my animation. He was so impressed that he offered me a job on the spot! He said his newly-formed media company was looking for animators and offered to hire me fulltime at $80,000 a year. I couldn't believe what I was hearing, and almost accepted it on the spot. But, I didn't.

Thankfully, I had enough sense to ask him to give me some time to consider his offer. I immediately consulted with my older brother Edwin. He was so proud and excited for me. Soon after, he started asking me some tough questions like: How long has this company been in business? Who are its clients? What are its core values? Have you seen samples of the type of work it creates?

All of these questions made sense, but then my brother dropped a real bombshell. He asked me, "If they are willing to pay you $80,000 without a four-year college degree, imagine how much more money you will be worth once you do graduate." That said, I reached out to Josh the next day and politely declined the offer. I did not want to drop out of school. However, I mentioned that I was flattered, and just wanted to finish my college degree before taking on any opportunities. I promised to keep in touch with him and hoped that he would consider me once I graduated.

After I graduated two years later, I reached out to Josh. I had done an incredible job of keeping in touch with him through the years. I informed him that I had just graduated and was looking for work. To my surprise, so was he! His company had gone out of business months before I called him. If I had accepted his job offer, I would have been out of work and without my four-year degree. To the say the least, I'm glad I turned the job down. Accepting that job would have changed my personal and professional life. That was when I learned that it was okay to tell a client "no."

PRICING YOUR SERVICES

Pricing your work is one of the biggest hurdles for even seasoned freelance entrepreneurs. What are your design services really worth? You can use the Graphic Artists Guild's book of price guides, but they may be outdated or not even relevant to your specific service. The thing to remember about pricing a project is that you have to make sure that it's worth your time and effort.

A few years ago, I added whiteboard animations to my design services. I had no clue what to charge. My circumstances at that moment dictated my pricing. Though I wasn't desperately in need of money, I was still looking to add more whiteboard animations to my online portfolio. I searched the price guide books, but my type of service was not listed.

When a client emailed me asking for my rates, I had to act fast. To buy some time, I asked her a list of mundane questions to keep her at bay long enough for me to get some ideas on what I should be charging. That's when I became an "undercover shopper." I called up several whiteboard freelance artists, and pretended that I was a client seeking their whiteboard services. I asked for their rates, turn-around times, allowed number of revisions, refund policy and much more. After calling five different artists, I used this information as a basis for pricing my own work. When the client finally reached out to me, I was well prepared to give her a quote.

Another approach is to look at other designers who are doing what you want to do. What are they charging for the same service? I don't normally suggest that you compare yourself to others. In this case, however, if you are both offering similar services then you can use those fees as a basis for your own pricing.

My absolute favorite strategy is to simply hold off on giving your client a quote, and be the first to ask them how much they have to spend. You still need to get price comparisons ("comps") ahead of time so that you make an informed decision once the client gives you their budget though not everyone lists their prices online. Pricing can of course change depending on the situation, the project specifications, and on who the client actually is.

NEGOTIATING YOUR PRICING

When you price your design services, be prepared to negotiate your pricing. Sometimes the negotiation process goes fairly easily. The client knows what they want, then they agree to your prices, pay your deposit, and you and the client work happily ever after. Other times, it requires more finesse.

The ideal situation is for the client to tell you how much they want to spend before you tell them how much you will charge. The reason for this is because they might be willing to spend more than you were going to charge them. In other situations, the client may not have a clue what it wants to pay or it simply wants the lowest possible rate for the highest possible quality.

Here is an actual transcript from a conversation that I had with a client. It started off with a request for a quote for a logo design, and I managed to turn it into something much larger by "upselling" my services. Fast food restaurants do it all the time when you ask for a burger, and they ask if you want fries and a Coke with that order. That's an upsell. I have concealed the client's name for obvious reasons.

Client: I am looking for a graphic designer to make a logo for my company. How much do you charge?
Me: Well, there are many different factors in what makes up the price of a logo. For example, how complex will the logo design be? When is your deadline? Do you want a text logo, graphic logo, mascot logo or a combination of all three? Do you have a style guide

or some references of the type of logo you want? How you will you be using the logo – online and print?

Client: We definitely need a logo for our website, flyers, and business cards

The most important part of the negotiation to me is the upsell. Notice my reply where I offer multiple services on top of just the logo that was requested.

Me: Sorry to interrupt, do you have marketing materials designed?

Client: No, not yet.

Me: OK, no problem. I can add that to the quote as well. I create all kinds of marketing and promotional materials as well as animated marketing videos and explainer videos. Don't worry, I got you covered! Once we begin working on the logo, it will be an easy transition to incorporate it into the marketing materials. But forgive me, please continue.

Client: Oh yes, no problem, thanks for mentioning that because we would like an explainer video as well. We are looking to have the logo completed within 2-3 weeks. I know that's not a lot of time. Is that doable?

Me: Yes, of course it is. To start, can you tell me which type of logo you are seeking? Text, graphic, mascot or a combo of the three?

Client: We definitely want a graphic with some text on it.

Me: Do you want the logo stacked, horizontal, or circular? Also, will you   need an additional app icon version of the logo? It might be a good idea to have at least two different versions of the logo, like stacked and horizontal versions so that you have the ability to place it on multiple objects.

Client: No, horizontal is fine. How much will that cost?

Me: Let me ask you this, what is your total budget for this project?

Client: Well, I don't know. It's our first time.

Me: I totally understand and I am here to help you through the process every step of the way. The reason I ask for your total budget is because there are different tiers to the type of logo design packages I can offer. So, if you give me a ballpark estimate of your budget, I can let you know what options you will have available. In an ideal world, how much would you like to spend?
Client: In an ideal world? Like $400.

Basic business negotiation theory states that the first offer given is usually not the client's maximum budget - it's more like their lowest. Before you respond to the $400 offer, consider whether or not this number matches the comps for graphic logo designs that you've researched. You should especially consider whether this amount is acceptable for you. If the number is too low for you, you still have some negotiating to do. Back to the transcript:

Me: Oh wow, $400 is very low for the type of design service you are requesting. My typical rate for this kind of work starts at $750.

Now, at this point three things can happen. The client could say no, this is too expensive; they can try to talk me down; or, they accept the price I propose. Although not the case with this client, clients sometimes will respond by saying that in an ideal world their budget is $3,000 or some absurd amount that was way more than you were going to charge. This is why you want to try to get them to throw a number out first.

It's a great idea to create a rate sheet that lists the pricing for the different types of services you offer. This way you can give the client an expensive option, a medium-priced option and a low-priced option. Always give the client options. After the client and I negotiated on a price for the logo, I ended up getting them to commit to an animated explainer video and a logo. Remember, their original budget was $400 and I managed to turn it into a $7,500 project!

CONTRACTS AND ARTIST'S AGREEMENTS

This is the most important part of any business deal that you make. Whether it's a freelance gig, a full-time job, or a book deal, you need a written contract that details the work, pricing, payment schedule, delivery dates, etc.

There are times where you may be asked to draw up a contract. In other cases, the client may provide you with an agreement to sign. PLEASE READ YOUR CONTRACTS! This will save you so much time, confusion and pounding headaches. Admittedly, there are some contracts that are incredibly hard to understand. Trust me when I tell you though that it is well worth the investment to have an attorney review your contracts and to get their approval before you sign anything.

If you have to draft the contract, keep it simple but be concise. Know what your limits are, what terms you are okay with, and clearly state them for your client to understand. It should be an agreement that is tailored to the project that you will be working on.

Again, every case is different. Most clients want to own the intellectual property rights for the work you create especially branded logos and mascots. You will need to negotiate these rights up front or risk losing the client. Communicate your terms clearly as part of your deal.

Don't wait until the very last minute to mention that all the work the client will pay for will remain your property. To be absolutely clear on this point, you may want to consult with an intellectual property lawyer to best protect your intellectual property rights. As I note elsewhere in this book, I've fought that battle and it's exhausting!

When the client provides its own contract and you don't understand all of the provisions, get the contract in front of a lawyer. If you can't afford to hire one, search for pro-bono attorneys - they're out there. If you're in California, California Lawyers for The Arts (https://calawyersforthearts.org/) can help. The Small Business Administration (www.sba.gov) may also have some pro-bono links as well. While retaining a lawyer to review the contract can sometimes make or break your deals, consider it insurance against making potentially serious mistakes.

THE SCHOLASTIC CONTRACT

In 2018, after Scholastic offered me a publishing deal for my children's book, it first sent me an informal agreement outlining some of the key points of the pending contract. I read the email about 100 times before I finally responded since I couldn't believe what I was reading. This was finally happening! Still, a lot changed from the terms in the informal agreement in that I was originally given. When I received the contract, I understood very little of it. I knew then that I needed to get this in front of a lawyer immediately.

Subsidiary rights, film rights, royalty amounts, merchandise rights, and other intellectual property rights were some of the key things that I wanted to fight for. When I first got the contract, of course, I just wanted to sign on the dotted line. This is Scholastic, the major children's book publisher of the world and publisher of the Harry Potter books!

Posing with Clifford at Scholastic Headquarters, Sept. 2018.

Once I came down from that high, I knew that I had to be smart about how I approached this deal. On the advice of my mentor, Gerald Chertavian, and my Small Business Development Center mentors, I sought out an entertainment lawyer. After I got on the phone with my attorneys, I had them review the contract. Before they responded with their thoughts, they asked me –

"Regarding your intellectual property, what rights are you willing to give up and what parts are non-negotiable? Before we can make any changes to the contract, you need to call Scholastic and be straight up with them about what your terms are. In our experience, this could be a deal breaker. They might walk away. If you're willing to take that risk, we are here to help."

It was the scariest call that I have ever had to make, and I still remember dialing the number. My heart was pounding so hard that I swore that Andrea heard it over the phone. As we spoke, I got straight to the point. I read off my list of requests. The phone fell silent. She responded by reminding me that I was a first-time author, and she could not guarantee that Scholastic would be able to grant all of my requests.

I didn't hear back from Andrea for almost two weeks. During the silence, I lost weight, couldn't eat, and I sure couldn't sleep. At the time, I was doing some freelance work at DC Collectibles Studio in Burbank, and was literally a zombie walking around the office. I was preparing to accept the fact that I might have just blown the biggest deal of my career.

When Andrea called me back to tell me that Scholastic had accepted most of my terms (higher royalties and I got to keep the majority of rights), I was absolutely overwhelmed. But that wasn't the best part of it. After all the negotiations were done and the contract (which had undergone several revisions) was signed, Andrea emailed me a quick note to say that she had so much respect for how I conducted myself like a professional and fought for what I wanted.

She commented that most people in my position would have just signed the contract. This experience would be the basis for all of my future contract negotiations. In business, sometimes you need to be willing to risk it all.

Walking with Andrea during our meeting in Sept. 2018.

Chapter Five
MANAGING CLIENTS

Learn how to manage your temper when your client loses theirs.

WORKING WITH CLIENTS

Sometimes working with clients can be difficult to manage. You're going to be dealing with so many different people and personality types. The secret to keeping clients happy is to maintain impeccable communication with them. Keep them updated at all times! If you're running late, let them know. If you need a break, let them know. Any moments of silence - lack of communication - will cause the client to develop fears such as "what if the artist just took my money and ran away."

It's a legitimate concern as many unsuspecting clients have been swindled by crooks posing as freelancers. The crooks will ask for a deposit and then disappear. Keeping in constant contact with your client will alleviate such potential worries for them. Here are a few tips that you can use to help you maintain a healthy working relationship with your clients:

- **Give them options:** Sometimes a client doesn't know what they want until you show them. Always give them two to three samples to choose from. It puts the power in their hands.

- **Set boundaries:** Make sure to let the client know what days and hours you work. If not, clients will call you on the weekends or holidays, and expect you to pick up the phone or respond to their many emails.

- **Ask for a reference point:** When the client wants to create a certain look, ask them to send you sample photos, links or videos. You want to get as close to the client's vision as possible from the start. This way there are so surprises when you deliver samples.

- **Get a deposit:** Never start a project until you get a deposit. This way if anything goes wrong, you can keep the deposit as the "kill fee" if client terminates the job. Sometimes a client wants a small sample to prove that you are the right fit for the job. Use discretion with this type of request. At other times, clients may ask for just enough so that they can use your sample as part of their actual production.

- **Do your research:** Whether you're dealing with a big business, small business or an individual, you want to look them up ahead of time and see what type of projects they have done in the past. See what their social media posts are about. Are they on Linkedin.com? When you apply for a job, employers do this to you to learn more about your character. Flip the script, and learn more about the client to see if it's a good fit for you as well.

- **Say Thank You:** Let the client know that you appreciate their support in the beginning, middle and end of the project. It will put a smile on their face and increase the chances of them returning to you for additional work in the future.

- **Don't give your business to someone else**: When a client asks you to send them some samples of your work, do not send samples through your social media site. Instead send them through your personal blog or your website. (You do have a website, right?) Social media pages are like a digital circus. Regardless of the site, there tend to be so many distractions, ads, videos, and other exciting content that it may distract the client from the reason you sent them there in the first place. You can easily lose a client to your competitors. Send them to your website!

- **Sign on the dotted line:** Make sure that you and your client have read and signed your artist's contract before you start work or send them an invoice. Hash out all of the details of the engagement and reflect those details in the contract before you start the project so that both parties are clear on the expectations for that engagement.

- **Avoid clients who pay with "great exposure":** When you are able to pay your mortgage or rent with "great exposure," then I would suggest you consider taking this as a method of payment. Otherwise, stay away from clients who promise you that their job will give you great exposure. If they really cared that much about your career, they would pay you with money like they do everything else.

- **Set daily goals:** To maximize your time, create a daily prioritized list of tasks that you need to complete. Don't overwhelm yourself with 50 tasks. List the top three things you want to accomplish that day. Get into a routine of accomplishing smaller goals, and this in turn will help you in accomplishing your larger goals.

- **Mandatory Self Care:** Most freelance artists spend many hours a day sitting down in front of a screen. Get up, turn off your gadgets, and go out to get some exercise. Read a book in the park, go on a date night, and especially eat and sleep regularly. Treat your business as a regular 9-5 job if you're doing it fulltime. If it's part-time or just a hobby, make sure you're still scheduling time for your health and well-being. There is no dollar amount on earth that is worth sacrificing your health for.

- **Learn the client's social media habits**: Ask your existing or prospective clients what social media platforms they use and how frequently they use them. Learn their habits so that you can post your content during times when they will be online to see it.

TURNING LEMONS INTO LEMONADE

As a freelancer, you will have some amazing clients and you will have some incredibly frustrating clients. What do you do when your client is upset? How should you handle their anger and frustration?

First understand that the client is not always right. However, if you're at fault then you need to own up to your mistakes. Think of ways to reconcile with the disgruntled client. Failure to do this may result in your reputation being ruined as word gets around that you screwed up the client's job. I'll admit it - I have had a few disgruntled clients due to some of my own mistakes.

One of those mistakes occurred in 2007 when I was commissioned to work on a website for one of my favorite clients, an incredibly talented DJ from Colorado named DJ Chonz. (Check him out at Djchonz.com). Prior to this work for hire, I had already worked for him and members of his crew for two years.

Frankly, I am not a web designer and realized that I had clearly bitten off more than I could chew. It took me months just to get a sample to him. He wasn't happy and rightfully so. He expressed his disappointment, and asked me to refund his money for work that had not been delivered. It was a huge embarrassment, but I refused to let it end that way.

I refunded his money, then offered to design party flyers for any events he had, free of charge, for the next three months. That month, DJ Chonz asked me to design a flyer for a major New Year's Party event. I knew that I was not going to get paid, but I had to work harder than ever if I was going to regain his trust.

When I delivered the flyer, DJ Chonz loved it so much that I received a notification of payment from him a short while later. I had redeemed myself! To this day, DJ Chonz remains a good friend and still one of my favorite clients. I had turned the proverbial lemon into lemonade.

Anytime you're dealing with a client, your goal shouldn't be to just complete the current commission. Instead it should also be your goal to build a relationship with the client so that when they need new work, you become the first person who comes to their mind.

ORGANIZE YOUR BUSINESS –
SOLE PROPRIETORSHIP VS. LIMITED LIABILITY CORPORATION

I am not a lawyer nor am I a tax accountant. As a freelancer, however, I can tell you that you want to make sure that you have the right business structure set up as this will help you avoid some future headaches. Depending on how big you intend to grow your business, you may want to get legal and tax advice on how best to organize your freelancing business.

I won't get into all of the different types of business structures that you can set up because if you're just starting out, there really are only two structures to choose between: A sole proprietorship (Sole Prop) or a Limited Liability Company (LLC). There are some key differences between the two that I have experienced since I have used both in the past. Both have their pros and cons.

A sole prop is cheaper and quicker to set up – just put your name on the door. In some states, though, you may have to register the name and get a business license. The cost of setting up an LLC can cost as much as $700 or more for the initial filing. You then must file annual reports and, depending on what state you're in, you may have to pay an annual franchise tax fee. At this writing, California's franchise tax is $800 a year whether you make money or not! With a sole prop, on the other hand, you're only paying income taxes through your individual tax returns.

You can find more details on how to form an LLC by reviewing your state's "Secretary of State" website. For example, the link to the California Secretary of State's "Business Entities" page is at https://www.sos.ca.gov/business-programs/business-entities/. Another critical point: you'll have to verify the availability of your proposed LLC name through the Secretary of State's office before you actually form the LLC.

As a freelancer, I have found more advantages being an LLC because of the types of freelance contracts that I have obtained with colleges and universities. Many of these clients will only do business with companies that have an IRS-issued tax identification number. Your LLC obtains a tax identification number upon your filing the pertinent paperwork. (Go to www.irs.gov for more information.) A sole prop, however, cannot be issued a tax identification number.

Another big difference is that an LLC provides you with more legal protection than a sole prop. For example, if your LLC goes into debt or is sued by an angry client, only your company assets will be exposed as long as you operate LLC business separately from your personal assets. In sharp contrast, a sole prop owner is "all in." Thus, if you I get sued or go into debt, all of your personal and business assets (house, car, property, personal bank accounts, etc.) can be in jeopardy.

The key in making the right decision here is to do your research. You can start at www.sba.gov, the Small Business Administration's website. I am not trying to sway you either way here because every situation is different. You should certainly consult with your business and financial specialists for a better idea of the type of business structure that is best for your freelance business. These specialists can help you navigate through the most common issues that small business owners face, including taxes and personal liability exposures.

WIN THE FIGHT WITH A COPYRIGHT (C)

It's been said that when someone steals your work, it's the sincerest form of flattery there is. Speaking from experience, I completely disagree with that. I have had my work ripped off several times and it's extremely upsetting, not flattering. Copyright is your first line of defense here.

Copyrighting your work is quick and simple under US law. Somewhere in the work, you need to include a form of copyright notice such as "(c) Heroes of Color LLC 2019". This puts the world on notice that this is your work. No registration is required, but registration is a good idea to ensure that your copyright is known to the public. In addition, registration entitles you to additional types of damages if you do have to sue someone for copyright infringement later.

Registering the copyright for your design is relatively cheap and simple. You can do this by going to the US Copyright's Office at www.copyright.gov, and completing the online form. You can expect to pay a small filing fee but this small investment can save you thousands of dollars if someone steals your design and you have to go to court. Please consult with a copyright attorney if you have reservations about registering the copyright yourself. Note, too, that you will be required to "deposit" a copy of the "work" you are registering the copyright for when you register.

Understand, however, that copyright law protects your expression, and not the idea for that latest design that you have created. Obtaining a copyright also won't stop anyone from stealing your design. The copyright will however help you win a copyright infringement court case. If you're lucky enough to actually catch the person who stole your work, contact an attorney right away. Do not reach out to the business or individual who ripped you off. Let the attorney handle it from that point on. And, yes, I have my own horror story here.

In 2008, I contacted an attorney because one of my Dominican cartoon character designs was ripped off by a calling card company. I couldn't afford an attorney, but the attorney agreed to take my case on a contingency fee basis. A contingent fee means that you only pay the attorney a percentage of the amount recovered if you win the case in court or reach a settlement. It has to be a pretty open and shut case in order for the attorney to agree to this. They do not want to take the risk in investing the time if they don't think they have a solid chance of winning. The case dragged on for a year before I finally reached a $14,000 settlement. The resemblance was uncanny. My original artwork is on the left. The infringed work is on the right.

The crazy thing was that while the calling card case was going on, I found out that I was being ripped off by another company in Puerto Rico. This one was huge. They manufactured a series of keychains, magnets, cups, stickers, and other merchandise with one of my Puerto Rican cartoon characters. What made this case difficult was that the company had thousands of pieces of merchandise created in China, and then sold them to stores all along the US East Coast. Between the investigations by my attorney and myself, we found over a dozen stores selling merchandise with my characters on it. Unfortunately, it got to be very expensive for me to pay the attorney.

HEREDIADESIGNS.COM

But wait! While all of this was going on, yet another company decided to rip me off by putting one of my Jamaican characters on their Jamaican food truck! It would seem that my multicultural cartoon series was in high demand. This wasn't flattery. Instead this was frustrating, agonizing and expensive.

For us designers, this is unfortunately just part of the territory. If someone wants your design bad enough, they will find a way to take it. One of the best tools I have used to my advantage was my network. After the first court case took place, I put out the word to everyone: "If you see any artwork out there that looks like mine, and it turns out that they infringed on my copyrights and I win the court case, I will cut you a check." This was the only reason I found out about the other two cases. In essence I had people all over the East Coast keeping an eye out on my intellectual property for me.

Chapter Six

DELIVERING SUCCESSFUL PROPOSALS

PROBLEM SOLVE, PRACTICE, PITCH, REPEAT!

One of the best pieces of advice I got early on in my freelancing career was **"If you use small bait, you catch small fish. If you use large bait, you catch large fish."** In the case of a freelance artist, writing a proposal is what I consider large bait that will help you land higher paying clients. Proposals typically target businesses, not individuals. At their core, proposals offer creative solutions - your design services – that will explain how a business can solve a problem it may be experiencing.

When you're making a pitch to an organization, you have only a few seconds to get its attention. If you start off by rambling on about how great you and your products are, you will lose them pretty quickly. Remember, an organization doesn't hire freelance designers because of your awards or products and services. An organization hires you based on your proposed solutions to its problems. For that reason, your proposal needs to be an attention-grabbing summation of how your services will solve their problems. A quick opening sentence can help **"bait the hook."** For example:

"In this proposal, I am going to show you how your company can increase its revenue by 50% by leveraging your social media pages with our new app."

It's also important to note that proposals require a lot of behind the scenes footwork. Not all proposals are created equal either, so while you may create a template that you can work from, every client has different needs. Don't try any short cuts on these proposals. Instead do the hard work! Your efforts will pay off big time when a company sees that you understand their needs. One great way to really increase your chances of landing that client is to offer the client multiple options with three different price packages. Now you've given them an opportunity to negotiate with you rather than just say "no" to your proposal.

If you're having trouble figuring out what problems the company is trying to solve, look at its history. What programs or services has it produced in the past and were they successful? The more you learn about your target client, the easier it will be to put a proposal together. A key fact here: a company is rarely going to reach out to you and ask you to put something together unless you initiate interest in solving their problem.

Think about what problems your services can solve. What organizations would benefit the most from your services? I saw instant growth in my business the minute I started targeting companies versus individuals. Whatever you do, make writing proposals an integral part of your business.

IDENTIFY THE PROBLEM

You might be thinking: how am I supposed to know what issues a company is trying to solve? The first clue is to look at their mission statement. Other times, company job titles will clue you into what the employees are tasked with solving or improving. For example, if an art gallery prospect holds the title of "Diversity Art Curator," then you could propose an incredible, multicultural art installation with some of the most talented, diverse artists you can find.

Another approach is to simply ask a target client "What are three of the top challenges that your gallery is working to improve upon?" Once you are aware of the issues the client is looking to solve, you are in a better position to propose a creative solution.

PROPOSE YOUR SOLUTIONS

Ask yourself what types of creative services you can provide with your current skill sets, gifts, and talents. This could range from art therapy, youth engagement, art workshops, and mentoring start-ups to beautifying a city with murals or even creating educational animations that promote positive representation in a community or school lacking in diversity.

In reality, that last one is actually one of my objectives with my "Heroes of Color" web series. Hopefully you can see how I can take that objective and pitch it successfully to schools struggling with lack of diversity in population and curriculum. Bottom line here: identify your strengths and then use them to strengthen your clients' needs or weaknesses.

TYPES OF DESIGN PROPOSALS

Your proposals should be unique to the client you are submitting it to. You can use that proposal as a guide for the next proposal you create, but it should not be a cut-and-paste type proposal for everyone because not every business has the same problem. Here are a few types of proposals that I have put together in the past:

- Instruct a college workshop
- Teach art classes at a community center or school
- Host a screening at a museum
- Create a new line of gift card designs
- Paint a mural in the lobby of a clothing store
- Create an immersive art show
- Pitch a new animation series
- Conduct a crowdfunding campaign

In all of these proposal situations, I first had to verify that my services would be the solution to these issues. In most cases, the client's mission statement was all I needed to get started. Once I made a connection with someone internally, I was able to start inquiring as to who the right contact person would be.

Believe me, nothing is more frustrating than making a pitch to the wrong person. Find out who the person is that's in charge of reviewing proposals. Avoid pitching blindly. Instead, try to develop a relationship with your client. Proposals will require other research as you want to make sure that your proposal speaks directly to the client's needs.

EXERCISE #5 – CREATE A PITCH PROPOSAL

Based on your design services, choose a design proposal category. Find an organization that would benefit from your services. Carefully review its mission statement. Does the organization's mission statement align with your own values? If it's a match, look for a contact person. If you cannot find the email of the point of contact listed on the website, give the client a call. Ask who would be the best contact person to pitch an idea or event to. Share your proposal with others before you send your pitch to that client.

THREE KEY POWERS OF PERSUASION

In the summer of 2018, I developed an art program for kids aged 8-17, called "Junior Artrepreneurs." It's an art program designed to turn young artists into entrepreneurs. My objective was to bring the program to elementary schools as an afterschool program. However, I needed to find a way to test the class and see if it worked.

An opportunity fell into my lap when I met a woman at my local coffee shop. It turned out that she was the youth ministry director for a local church, and was looking for a new program related to the arts that focused on engaging youth who had become disconnected from the church. This wasn't my original objective but, with a few minor adjustments, I reworded the program's mission to align with hers. I clearly outlined the solution by leading with all of the benefits of the program. Below are actual pages from that proposal.

DOWNLOAD SAMPLE PROPOSAL

Scan this QR Code to access the Junior Arts Proposal packet.

Several things worked in my favor in making this pitch. The most powerful was the ability to pitch the workshop in person before presenting the proposal. This process allows you to really leverage the three key powers of persuasion: Trust, Logic and Emotion. Establishing trust is crucial not just in obtaining a client, but in keeping them.

People want to work with someone who is credible, likable, and makes them feel comfortable. Teach a class, write a book (but not this one!), or write a guest post on a reputable website in your industry. Any of these will help position you as an industry expert who people can trust.

Keep in mind, too, that the proposal has to make logical sense to them. Speak with confidence - you have to believe it in order to achieve it! You're not selling them a dream, but you should be presenting a flawless, factual presentation. Your proposal must capture their imagination. You don't have much time to get the client's attention, so you must get them emotionally engaged early on. Take them on an emotional journey to help close the deal with an impactful, personal story. Remember, facts tell, but stories sell. Here is how I used the powers of persuasion during my pitch for my Junior Arts proposal:

Trust: My professional credentials and activism for youth made me appealing to youth ministry director because she felt that I understood her demographic well. I was genuine and confident when I spoke.

Logic: My proposal made sense to the youth ministry director because of all of the valuable life lessons the youthful audience would gain from my workshop. These benefits included business knowledge, financial independence, family bonding, and a student art show for participants to sell their work to the community. Lead your proposal with benefits!

Emotion: I shared a personal story of how I personally disconnected from the church years ago, and how creating artwork for a religious summer retreat brought me closer to God and therefore my family. I showed that my solution works and that I'm living proof of that.

You can see now that the proposal was crafted specifically for the church, and how it was a perfect fit. After I conducted the actual workshop, I gathered real data and used it to strengthen the proposal packet for the next time I proposed the class.

PROSPECTING FOR CLIENTS

The proposals you create will get stronger each time you present them, especially if the proposal targets the same demographic. Sometimes you will have all the elements of your proposal ready, and just need to make minor tweaks before you are ready to present it. On other occasions, you will need to have the wisdom to spot a potential opportunity developing during your conversation with a client, and then speak to the prospective client as if you already have a proposal prepared specifically for them. Remember, good things don't come to those who wait, they come to those who hustle.

Recently, I pitched a one-day event for a proposed Black History Month event in February of 2020 at the Schomburg Research Center in Harlem. I had no idea how I was going to do this, and didn't plan it out thoroughly. Still, I knew how much it would cost and the resources I needed to get it done. I scheduled a call with the director of the center to make a soft pitch over the phone. It is important to note that this was a very "warm" lead since I had already worked with the director before.

In January 2018, the Schomburg Research Center invited me to give a 45-minute talk and screening of my "Heroes of Color" videos during the Black Comic Book Festival. It was an incredible experience and one which landed me some great news coverage as well as an NPR radio interview. Clearly my new proposal was going to be read by people familiar with my prior work. Realizing the success of the previous speaking engagement, I was now looking for a way to "supersize" my services. It's common practice in business to extend lots of energy in trying to get new clients. What we really need to realize is that it's much easier to get repeat business from clients you have already worked with versus spending the time and money on trying to land a brand-new client. You just have to find a way to repackage your previous services, or add something new to them.

I asked the director of the Schomburg Research Center candidly about some of her programs' biggest obstacles. I wanted to propose something that would specifically address her problems. She mentioned that their teen audience was only interested in technology instead of history. She also mentioned that they had a digital gallery museum without any digital installations to put up.

Obviously, she had just given me the solutions to her problems. I just needed to paint a picture for her on how my services could totally resolve those issues, and quickly went into my soft pitch. That pitch: I would host a screening of a new "Heroes of Color" episode, followed by an immersive art gallery show where teens had to use their cellphones to find clues in the artwork using A.R. technology (Augmented Reality). When their phone targeted a specific image, a video or audio would pop up on the user's cellphone screen.

For the digital gallery, I proposed several different immersive installations. The audience would be entertained, engaged, and educated. I understood the Center's problem, but more importantly, I provided a specific solution on how to solve it.

SELLING SOMETHING THAT DOESN'T EXIST - YET

Have you ever ordered an item that was only available via "pre-order or pre-sale?" I recently learned that, sometimes, this means that the product might not exist yet. The business owner sometimes uses "pre-sale" orders as a way to raise enough money to then manufacture the product. It's genius.

Keeping this in mind, I recently **"sold something that didn't exist."** I made a proposal to a professional development organization. This wasn't a "cold call" pitch. It was instead a warm lead because I had done business with that organization before. Back then, I was paid hourly. This time, I wanted a percentage per student enrolled.

The challenge: if I was going to take a bigger cut from the organization's profits, this deal had to make sense. I refined and repackaged the workshop as a comprehensive, three-week webinar series designed to help artists create a sustainable freelance business. I would handle everything and they would do...well, nothing. This was clearly a win-win situation for the organization that involved no risk or investment. I didn't need their facilities - just access to their students. The organization's director loved the idea and we scheduled a discussion the next day.

One minor problem: I had never done a webinar before! Quite frankly, I didn't know the first thing about creating a compelling webinar. What I did have was faith in my ability to learn how to create an engaging webinar. Remember, skills can be taught. Don't lose an opportunity because you lack the skills to execute the job. If you can't do it, hire someone who can help you or do it for you. This is often referred to as outsourcing.

LEARN FROM REJECTION

Like most things in life, the first time is always the most awkward. Don't worry: the more proposals you create, the stronger they will become. Once you understand that rejection is a part of the learning process, you won't take it personally when your proposals are turned down. Instead, you need to use that rejection as an opportunity to learn. You learn by asking for feedback on what you can do to strengthen the pitch or proposal.

In 2017, a proposal I put together was rejected. It was an animation design proposal for the Japanese American National Museum in Los Angeles. In my mind, I just knew that they would want my services. In reality, I didn't have a clue about what their specific challenges were or what the needs of the organization were. I moved forward with it anyway. I proposed a series of custom "Heroes of Color" animated episodes on the Nisei soldiers, a highly-decorated Japanese-American battalion that served in the U.S. Army in World War II.

All of my emails and cold call requests for a meeting were ignored. One of the people in my network, however, knew the director of the museum. The director and I exchanged a few emails before finally scheduling a date to meet. From the minute I walked in, I noticed the lobby was covered with images, videos and artifacts about the Nisei soldiers. My enthusiasm waited for me at the front door while I walked into the museum with a sullen look.

The meeting itself was a blur. When I met the director, she looked less than pleased to see me. She rapidly fanned through my six-page proposal without even looking at it once. Before I knew it, she was thanking me and rushing me out the door saying that they were not interested.

After I got home, I sent her an email thanking her for her time. At the end of the email, I asked if she could give me some feedback on what steps I could take in the future to strengthen any future proposals I might have for the museum. She responded with a list of points that I still use as a guide till this day. In fact, her email response became the basis of my 10 elements of a winning proposal.

THE 10 ELEMENTS OF A WINNING PROPOSAL

I realize that there are several different ways to present proposals. The following were steps that I used and that worked for me. You can also find some templates online to help guide your own proposal drafting. The important thing is to make sure you are only using the bits and pieces that speak directly to your client's needs. Here are 10 things that you want to keep in mind when you are creating your proposals:

1. *Research your client before you pitch.*
2. *Provide a clear solution as to how your services will solve the client's problem.*
3. *Highlight the powers of persuasion: Trust, Logic and Emotion.*
4. *Lead with your benefits, then back them up with features.*
5. *When providing cost proposals, always provide two to three different price options.*
6. *Include clear timeline or estimated time of completion for your proposed project.*
7. *Include a contract with the proposal that the client can sign*
8. *Learn about any previously successful partnerships the client has had in the past.*
9. *Present proposals to the decision-makers, not to their assistants.*
10. *Get feedback from other entrepreneurs before you pitch.*

PRICING YOUR DESIGN PROPOSAL

One of the most difficult things for freelancers to do is setting prices especially if it's a project that you've never worked on before. Every proposal you create will be unique to the client, so there are no set standards. However, here are four quick suggestions that you can use to help you create the most accurate quotes for your design proposals.

1. **Ask what the client's budget is:** The quickest way to price your proposal is to ask the client directly: how much do they have in the budget for your proposed services? The client will usually provide a low number. It's up to you if you want to accept it, modify your services to fit within their budget, or

negotiate a totally new number. Negotiating is part of the game so get used to it. (Re-review Chapter 4 on this point)

2. **Ask a similar business for pricing advice:** Show your proposal to a business that is similar to the one you are pitching to, and ask for their advice on pricing. You aren't pitching to them, so they might give you a more direct, honest answer. It's not coming out of their budget so they might even tell you if it's priced too high or too low.

3. **Ask another entrepreneur:** Get your proposal in front of another entrepreneur with more experience than you, and ask for advice. If you don't know of such people, start joining groups on social media and engage with them.

4. **Know the client's history:** Ask how much they have budgeted for previous proposals that are similar to yours. Make sure you are talking to the correct person who would have that information and who actually can negotiate a final price.

The Graphic Artists Guild publishes a book on suggested pricing based on the types of project you create. Ultimately, though, the price has to make sense to you. A few immediate things to consider in pricing are:

- Will it require travel, lodging, and meals? Will these costs be covered by your pricing?
- What are some your estimated costs for materials or supplies?
- How many hours of your time will it take you to prepare for the event or create the project?

I am sure that you can think of other factors to include in your pricing, but you get the point. Start outlining the immediate expenses that you will need to cover, and then add a salary factor to ensure you are getting paid. Make sure that the amount you charge doesn't just cover your expenses - you should be making a profit from this project, too. Otherwise, what's the point? You don't want to just get by, you want to get ahead.

MARKETING TECHNIQUES

WHAT IS MARKETING?

Marketing is made up of multiple ingredients such as advertising, branding, promotion, publicity, and sales. When these are all combined to help you meet a specific goal, that's marketing. Let's look at a freelance artist's fictional marketing campaign that will promote her services, and get her custom orders prior to her weekend event:

Advertising: The freelancer paints an incredible sign with caricatures and words saying "Master caricature artist coming to your theme park this weekend. Don't wait - place your custom orders now!"

Promotion: The freelancer puts the sign on top of her car and drives around town creating interest.

Publicity: If the car causes a major traffic jam of onlookers, the police come out to direct traffic. Better yet: the newspaper writes a story about "the car sign that stopped traffic."

Sales: People visit her website after reading that story in the newspaper and start requesting custom orders.

Branding: The freelancer puts her logo and website on all promotional materials that she hands to her paying customer. This could include stickers, pens, caps and t-shirts, etc.

Marketing: The freelancer planned all of the above!

Marketing isn't just about visibility. Successful marketing strategies are those that:

- Identify your Target Market
- Have a clear message to tell your target market
- Define what media outlets will be used to reach your target market
- Have a system in place to capture leads (contacts or potential customers)
- Have a system in place to convert these leads into sales
- Have the ability to deliver a memorable experience
- Keep customers coming back (retention), and
- Have a plan to continue generating referrals

Another consideration here: how visible are you to your target market? Your products and services should be easy to find on and off line. The more you stay in the public eye, the more opportunities you can create for yourself. When it comes to social media, not everyone who follows you or reads your posts will like, comment or share. They may be silently watching your posts. Don't worry about it - keep posting daily. Automated posting is the way to go. You can come up with the most incredible marketing strategy possible, but it means nothing if you don't put your tactics into action.

Since there are so many variables involved in constructing a marketing plan, one size does not fit all. You have to think about your budget, your time management, the resources you have available to you at the time, and who you've identified as your ideal customer. You'll also want to outline what your ultimate goals are for your marketing effort.

These variables will be different for every freelance artist, but the ultimate goal should be the same - to give your target market a call to action. There is some action that you want them to take after they have seen your advertisement or promotion. The more specific you are with the goals you want to achieve, the more precise your advertisements will be.

Keep it simple and be clear with your call to action. Test out the copy that you write in your ads by showing it to friends who "fit" your ideal target market and see if they get the message you were trying to convey. Clever marketing can be inexpensive so you can get creative with it. I have seen some low-cost chalk drawings on the sidewalks which were hilarious and memorable. If your marketing strategy has an emotional appeal, it's more likely to stick.

STRATEGY VS. TACTICS

The easiest way to describe the difference between the two is strategy is the plan while tactics are the actions you take to execute your plan. Put another way, your strategy is the ultimate objective or reason why you are launching the campaign. The tactics are the methods or tools that you use to obtain these objectives. Here is a quick example for a caricature designer:

Strategy:
- To become the most sought out caricature designer in the US.

Tactics:

- Design two free caricatures of celebrities a month and tag them
- Ask the celebrities to retweet those designs
- Ask friends to retweet the celebrity caricatures
- Use Twitter, Facebook, and Instagram to engage regularly while using automated posting via Hootsuite of previous caricature designs created.
- Create caricatures of radio personalities and music industry DJ's with high followings.

Once you develop your strategy, make sure that you are tracking it. If it's not working, change it. Remember, your goal isn't to market to everyone. You need to be very specific with who you are targeting. Once you have pinpointed the ideal client, you will be in a better position to talk to them.

Remember, too, that your ideal client isn't buying your product. Instead they are buying the result that your product will bring them. You're selling solutions to an existing problem. For example, someone who sells a big fat breakfast cereal spoon isn't really selling spoons. They are selling a way for you to pick up more food each time you put that spoon inside your bowl of cereal.

That's a great way to eat faster if you're always rushing to eat in the morning before rushing off to school or work. A fatter spoon might speed things up. The result is what they are sold on, not the product. Don't talk about how great your product is - talk about how great the customer will be after sampling your product. Here's a quick example of the "problem/solution" question:

- **Problem:** You know how artists are always starving because they can't find work?
- **Solution:** My freelance business workshop teaches artists how to become financially independent by teaching them how to monetize their gifts with the skillsets they currently have.

- **Proof:** Within a week of taking the workshop, two students had already secured new paying clients with the topics taught in the class.

COPYWRITING

Copywriting for sales is a skill that not everyone possesses. Use your headline as a starting point to entice your audience. How many times have the newspaper headlines stopped you in your tracks? Or, emails with subject lines that you just had to click on! Great copy is an essential part of a sale.

Emotion is probably the biggest driver of sales. Sales that trigger our guilt, love, fear, pride or greed all go to our emotions. The news media do an absolutely amazing job pumping fear into our minds. After a slight 4.5 tremor in Santa Clarita one August, the television and radio news outlets went on a rampage telling us how we needed to rush to the stores right now and get water, our earthquake kits, food, and flashlights.

I was only halfway dressed before I jumped into the car, and arrived to an absolute mad house at our local grocery store. You would have thought the world was coming to an end! Great sales copy that triggers emotions like this yields the best results. The top selling businesses move you to buy products based on at least one of these basic emotional triggers. It's a tactic that politicians are also very familiar with.

101 KILLER MARKETING TACTICS

I believe that marketing and self-promotion are two of the key ingredients needed to create new opportunities for yourself as a freelancer. What good is having incredible design services if no one is aware that you offer them? You have to get your offerings out into the open endlessly and repeatedly.

Be the best promoter of your brand. Wear your art, speak about your art, and promote your work every chance you get. Here are 101 clever ways to promote yourself and your design services. Some are free while others may require a small investment, but the best investment an entrepreneur can make is an investment in themselves.

It's important to mention that many of the items on this list of self-marketing and promotional ideas have led me to obtain new clients. So, here's the list, but don't feel like you have to try them all:

1. **Create a marketing plan:** Clearly outline your objectives for what you want to accomplish and create a plan for the steps you need to take to take action. No building has ever been constructed without a blueprint.

2. **Create your own website:** Update your webpage regularly. Add a blog page to enable you to post current events and projects that you are working on. Link your social networks sites on the website. If you don't already have a website, there are dozens of do it yourself websites that require no coding such as Weebly, Wordpress, and Wix, to name a few. When applying for freelance gigs, you want to ensure that you have a professional website built, preferably with the same URL as your company name. Even if you have a social media site, you want to bring people to your website and remove any distractions that can lead to your client clicking on someone else's social media ad or page.

3. **Business cards:** If you are a creative person, create a business card that someone will want to keep! You don't have to design the boring old, corporate cards. Remember you're not just creating a business card, you're creating a conversation piece.

4. **Cellphone covers:** People invest small fortunes into their cellphones. So should you, but don't rush out and buy the latest $1,000 phone. Instead just pay about $20 for a customized cellphone cover and promote your artwork on the case of your phone. You are making other people aware of your designs, and that cellphone cover can help spark conversations with prospective clients interested in your work. There are dozens of do-it-yourself printing sites like Redbubble.com that can handle this type of design job.

5. **Custom designed envelopes:** When was the last time you receive a personally handwritten letter with a custom designed envelope? Outside of Christmas, it's probably been a while. I know writing letters is a lost art form, but that's what makes it so special now. It's not the usual method of communication so it can help you stick out like a sore thumb. The objective here is never blend in. Best of all, you can customize each envelope to suit your target market.

6. **Yard Signs:** This is the go-to marketing platform for politicians that can be found strategically placed right off the freeways, yards of supporters, high traffic locations and more. It might not hurt to create a promotion in the style of a political ad, even if it's not an election year. They are pretty affordable to print (gotprint.com offers them at great rates), and you will be amazed how long these yard signs live undisturbed once placed in the ground.

7. **The elevator pitch:** It costs nothing! The idea is that you know your services inside and out. You already know how it will solve the potential problems of your clients. When you are faced with an unexpected opportunity to speak to a potential client about your services and the benefits of working with you, you must be ready to go without hesitation.

8. **Don't just like, Engage:** In order to get your brand recognized and trusted, you must be easily accessible and visible to the public. This requires posting regularly, sharing other people's posts, commenting, mentioning, tagging, liking, etc. There are dozens of networks to choose from. Use some or use all of them. Just make sure that you are actively engaging online. Oh yea, and make sure you get your contacts' emails and start building your own email list.

9. **Avatars:** Change your avatars regularly across all the social media networks that you use. You will be amazed how much engagement this sparks. This is a great chance to post your new headshot, new product picture, family selfie, etc.

10. **Background images:** Similar to the strategy of changing your avatars, do the same with your backgrounds or headers on Facebook and Twitter. Take every opportunity that you can to promote new

work, products or designs. Remember, every time you make a noticeable change, sites like Facebook send out alerts to your followers of that recent change.

11. **Customized background images:** While we are on the topic of background images, ask your friends or followers to change their avatars and backgrounds to images with your products or designs. Another option is to create a custom design for them that promotes your work. Having multiple people promoting for you will multiply your marketing efforts.

12. **Laptop promo's:** How often do we go to coffee shops, libraries or bookstores and see the glowing Apple logo on laptops around you? Often enough to know that instead of promoting other brands, you can use that same laptop cover to promote your own brand. Print up custom stickers or custom laptop skins with your work. Get into the habit of promoting your brand, not others'.

13. **Email signature:** If you're like me, you send out hundreds of emails a week. At the very bottom of your email you can customize your signature to show your name, website, and any other notable links you want to share with people. You can even add a small image to your email signature.

14. **Post video clips:** When you're posting your content online, remember that videos perform much better than photos or posts without any images. Get creative with this. You don't have to just use real live video clips. Instead use some of your own animation or custom-created GIFs. Try different things to see which ones perform best for you.

ANIMATED GIF

Scan this QR Code to view my animated gif used on twitter.

15. **Community announcement boards:** Avoid messy cork boards. Instead target the organized boards located at schools, coffee shops,

libraries, high-end grocery stores, and anywhere else that you can find your target markets.

16. **Explainer videos:** Having an explainer video helps your potential clients understand the benefits of your new products and services. If you're an animator, this is a must have video to add to your website. Keep it simple, but make sure it's effective. By having my own explainer video, I was hired to create over a dozen explainer videos for clients who wanted something similar to what I had. My experience has shown me that, more often than not, clients don't always know what they want until you show them.

EXPLAINER VIDEOS

Scan this QR Code to view one of my explainer videos.

17. **Digital freebies:** Proceed with caution on this one. Back when I was hooked on Twitter, I offered "free" custom name designs to influencers or people who had high engagements for their posts. I specifically targeted people whose fans loved the type of designs I created. I would make a deal with them first. Then I would ask them if I did a free design of their name, would they repost and tag me on it. These people rarely say no!

Once they posted my design, it usually resulted in hundreds of instant followers who loved the work. Often times, I was able to convert the new followers into paid freelance gigs. You must, however, be selective with who you choose to create free art for. Make sure this giveaway will benefit you both. Try building a rapport with them first. If you just do it blindly, they may not respond or repost it.

Digital freebie FAIL: Remember my previous warning to proceed with caution on this one? Here's the reason why. Imagine spending hours doing an amazing design for someone with a huge following. The hope is that this influencer will fall head over heels for your design and share it with their legion of followers. Well, that's not how it went down in my case. I created a text and cartoon design of Gal Gadot, the actress from the blockbuster movie "Wonder Woman." Unfortunately, the design went unnoticed and all I got from it was frustration. **Build a rapport with your influencer first!**

18. **Mention influencers:** Mentioning or tagging influencers in your post doesn't always go unnoticed. It's a great way to get them to view your designs and services. If they like it, they may retweet or follow you. It's a numbers game, so you have to keep at it, but it's a good look for you if they endorse you with a repost.

19. **Sticker bombs:** While I am not encouraging you to get out and start vandalizing anything, there are still some very hip businesses that welcome your posting your sticker design in their stores, counters, etc.

20. **Creative haircuts:** If you know a barber talented enough to cut designs on your next haircut, have them cut your logo or one of your designs on the back of your head! Hire a group of teens to attend an industry-related event, and pay to have all of their haircuts with your logo, website or designs.

21. **Guest postings:** Write an article on an industry-related site. Sites like Huffington Post, Inc.com, Entrepreneur, and Business Insider are just some of the companies that will accept your article if it fits their guidelines. If your article gets picked up, it gives you instant credibility and may lead to sales or new followers from the traffic your article generated.

22. **Workshops:** Create your own workshop related to your industry. You can offer to do it for free to help fill the room. This is a great way to position yourself as an expert in your field while networking and creating some potential leads.

23. **Enter contests:** There are dozens of online contests and challenges in existence. Why not enter a monthly creative contest related to your field? It's great way to gain visibility. If you win, you add another level of prestige to your services.

24. **Car Wrap:** If you drive to school or work every day, this could pay off for you big time. Use your car as a billboard. You sit in traffic for hours per week, and your car is parked for other periods of time. Advertise your product or design services with a unique car design wrap that motorists will not be able to ignore.

25. **Bumper stickers & car magnets:** If you don't have a huge budget for a car wrap, a bumper sticker or a magnetic car sign with your business information may be a more affordable option. Print up a few and ask your family and friends to put some on their cars, too.

26. **Apply for grants:** There are more and more artistic grants being awarded to individuals these days. Whether you're awarded the grant or not, sometimes the process of applying makes people aware of your work and often times sparks interest in your business. This in turn can help you can develop relationships that can ultimately lead to you getting funding.

27. **Exhibit at Comicon:** Attend the San Diego Comic Con or similar shows as a vendor. Get your own table or split one with another creative artist. This is the perfect way to test your products with an audience. You have the potential for selling your merchandise, building an organic fan base, and even getting hired for commissioned work.

28. **Street teams:** Attend an industry-related event, festival or parade and hire a group of people to wear matching shirts designed with your logo, website and cool image on it. The street team will get a lot of attention and as they engage with people and hand out your flyers. This in turn can encourage the crowd to visit your website for more examples of your work or to order custom work.

29. **Bookmarks:** People still love to read books. So why not create some bookmarks and give them away to your local public library, elementary school libraries, and bookstores? Add a great illustration, message and your website to the bookmark.

30. **Augmented reality:** From children's books, art installations, business cards or any other flat artwork, bring it to life using "augmented reality." Once users download an AR app (Artivive.com is the one I use in this book, but there are several others on the market) you can scan your piece of artwork which will be triggered when someone rolls their phone over it. Once it's triggered, you can command what you want the result to be by linking it to either more 2D pop ups, an animation or a video with full sound. This will add

an engaging piece of technology to any piece of artwork you make, and certainly captivate your audience enough to want to learn more about the works you create. To give you an idea of how this works, take a look at what happens when you hover your phone over my old business card. You must first download an app in order for it to trigger a video with sound directly on your phone.

Download "Artivive" from google play or iTunes. Open app, then hover your phone over this image to see how to make your printed images pop! Make sure the volume is up on your phone.

31. **Follow your target market:** Go to events where your target market will be in attendance. For example, DJ's and musicians almost always need graphic design services. If you design party flyers, logos, and other graphic design items, why not attend a DJ or HipHop conference and hand out dozens of your promotional design materials to all the musicians, rappers, DJ's or people in attendance. Chances are that your competitors won't be there, and you will have a room full of potential clients all to yourself.

32. **Tattoo sleeves:** Upload your work to companies like samples.com and get your own customized tattoo sleeve promoting your designs.

Others might actually want to buy this tattoo sleeve, but either way, it's a clever way to showcase your work.

33. **Creative packaging:** Presentation is everything. That said, how unique can you make your packaging for an event? Even if you just order some brown paper bags to give your clients when they buy an art print, why not draw something on the brown bag? Customize it in a way that makes you stand out among the rest of the vendors. Keep finding ways to make your business stick out like a sore thumb.

34. **Promotional materials:** Print up some pens, notepads, or other small giveaways with your website on them. If you can include some images, that's even better. Hand them out to your target market or in places where your target market will be. The materials should be cost effective and relevant to your design services.

35. **Word of mouth:** Nothing is better than free advertising. The more you put yourself out there, the more likely people are to talk about what you do. Sometimes it's as easy as telling people to tell their friends about your work. Like a drop of water in a still lake, the ripples that drop causes can spread farther than you know.

36. **Flyers:** These are so affordable these days that I would recommend that you create custom-designed flyers for specific events or specific services that you want to highlight. Create flyers (gotprint.com) that you can give to potential customers, flyers for industry events, and general flyers that work for any type of event, festival or gathering. Regardless, just make sure that you always have marketing material handy.

37. **Follow up's:** This is the key to closing deals with clients. Sometimes they forget to make a final decision or get distracted. Give them a friendly nudge by following up in multiple ways until they respond.

38. **Sponsor events:** One of the best ways to build brand awareness is to sponsor a sporting event in your local town. Costs may vary, but having a banner with your design and logo hanging at a football or baseball game is a great look. It shows that you support your local sports teams while providing exposure to your business.

39. **Venice Beach:** These legendary walls draw a constantly huge crowd. Painting graffiti designs pertaining to your business is a great way to build brand awareness. If you aren't a graffiti writer, link up with someone who is and hire them to design an entire side of the wall. The wall space is free!

40. **Customized restaurant kid's menus:** While restaurant companies have in house designers for this, you can always offer to design a free custom page that will be appealing to patrons and offer it as an additional coloring or activity page. Make sure to have your website address on it.

41. **Adult coloring pages:** This is something adults are into these days. Art therapy helped popularize the new wave of adult coloring books as a therapeutic practice. Libraries too have adopted this practice as well. Why not create some of your own designs and offer them for free to hospitals, art therapists, schools, etc.?

42. **Monthly email blasts**: Send email blasts to people that you know are into your work. Don't buy an email lists though - you want organic followers. They may not always respond, but they may be triggered by a message you put out that prompts them to commission you for work or to connect you with someone who needs your services. The idea is to stay fresh in their minds at all times.

43. **Referrals:** This is the new currency - getting people to refer your services. That way, they are doing all the hard selling for you. People do business with people who they trust. When you ask your previous clients to vouch for you, you are building a team of agents!

44. **Stay in touch:** Call your previous clients to say hello. If you don't have their number handy, send them a hello by email and make them aware of your latest accomplishments. It's one on one and more personal than an email blast.

45. **Create a tutorial:** This can be done as a video, or as a step-by-step illustration. We all love industry tips and tricks. Remember, regardless of the level of experience you have in your field, there are always people who know less than you do and are searching for ways to learn what you know.

46. **3D chalk artist:** Hire a 3D Chalk artist to create a fun scene in the park with your logo and design. Make sure it's in a public space – and legal! - where there is lots of foot traffic. Make sure that your website address is clearly visible. This will form crowds and lots of attention. That's great for you and your chalk artist.

47. **Work in progress:** Create a "work in progress" video of yourself working on a design. You can use screen capture software such as "Screenflow" to record your computer screen as you work. People love to see your process of design, so use it to your advantage.

48. **Infographics:** Well-designed infographics can be educational and even help set you up as an expert in your field. Use statistics, fun, or comedy. Well-designed infographics are more likely to be shared by others online so take your time in making one. For inspiration, Google "infographics" – you'll be surprised at the possibilities for your business.

49. **Join a business group:** There are any number of online and offline business groups that you can join. It's a great way to network and get your name out there. Meetup.com, Linkedin and Facebook groups can help you find groups in your industry or fields of interest.

50. **Text marketing:** It is estimated that 97.5% of text messages are read within five seconds. That's a huge response rate. However, be careful with this one since there is nothing more annoying than to get text messages from someone you don't know. Your best bet: start texting your digital ads designed for mobile to people that you do know. They can help you spread the word within their close circle. Sending text messages to strangers can give your brand a bad name.

51. **Create a Top 10 list:** Everyone loves a list. List things related to your industry (tools, software, blogs, design hacks, etc.) Be creative and make people want to share it. You can also dress your list with some great illustrations or humor.

52. **Create catchy titles:** You can lead people to read an article or a book just by the title or subtitle you use. Create 5-10 attention grabbing titles for your blog, stories, or posts, and then choose the best one to see how people respond to it.

53. **Wear your own shirts:** There is no better billboard than your own body! You can give them away to family members and friends and have them help you promote your brand. Hire models to wear them. Even better, seek out the PR people of celebrities and see if they will wear your shirt.

54. **Meet clients in person:** Whenever possible, look for an opportunity to build your relationship with a client by having in person meetings. This builds trust while helping to reduce the amount of miscommunication that can occur by exchanging information via emails. Treat your client to a coffee or tea at the local coffee shop. It's a small gesture, but a little bit goes a long way.

55. **Create an app:** The convenience of online shopping has led to the financial success of many businesses. People are using mobile apps for online shopping, playing online games and so much more.

56. **Host a webinar:** If you have a topic, tutorial, or tips you want to share with people, host a free webinar. It's a great way to build your audience and also practice selling your services and products to prospective clients. Search some free options like EzTalks Webinar, Google+ Hangouts, or Skype. If that goes well for you, then you can upgrade to paid webinar services that allow you to handle payments as well as provide more capacity to allow more people to attend your webinars. Some of the paid webinar sites include GoToWebinar, ClickMeeting, and Webex. A webinar can be fun, and it also helps to set you up as an expert in your field.

57. **Hand written cards:** Don't just wait for the holidays - pick up a pen, lined paper and write someone a hello note. In this digital age, getting a personalized letter would be much appreciated and completely unexpected. People may not remember what your letter or card said, but they won't forget how they felt just to receive it.

58. **Comparison charts:** These should be visual side-by-side charts that compare people, music, products or services. For example, there is an amazing infographic online that explains the differences between

a geek and a nerd that is absolutely brilliant. Create something about your business or skillset that is so visually stunning and humorous that it will trigger people to want to share it.

59. **Virtual agents:** This is covered in much more detail in Chapter Eight. Virtual agents are websites where you can set up art profiles in websites like Guru.com or Upwork.com and create a portfolio. Whenever a client is seeking to hire a creative artist that matches your profile, you are notified via email. These sites essentially find work for you while you sleep.

60. **Client testimonials:** This is your social currency. Your credibility goes way up when you can get other people to talk about how great your designs are. Ask them to leave comments on your social media pages. If you use videos, make sure they leave comments on your videos as well. Linkedin.com is also great for this feature.

61. **Host an event:** Host a get together! Invite your target market, and partner with a non-profit or organization to make it mutually beneficial to you both. The event should be free to the community, and have some form of entertainment like a DJ playing music in the background. Make sure you are clear about what the event is such as an exclusive animation screening, a new art exhibition, etc. Invite local media and ask them to write an article about your event and you.

62. **Create a commercial:** Work with a team to develop a 15-30 second commercial for your product or services. Unlike an explainer video, you want to have actual footage to edit. Hire some skilled students to shoot your commercial. Make it memorable - think Super Bowl commercials.

63. **Social proof:** This one is a bit more elaborate. It may even require participation from a local store or coffee shop. The idea: you want to create a public stunt or prank, something that promotes your service or design in a fun and unique way. In addition, you'll want to record video or pictures of people reacting positively to your product.

64. **Partnerships:** Find out how you can partner up with an organization that has a mission similar to yours. If it's a good fit, you can both

promote one other's projects. Think about how you can solve a problem for the organization before you think about how it can benefit you.

65. **Brochures:** Create a brochure outlining your services. These are pretty affordable and make great marketing materials to drop off at events and local shops.

66. **Scheduled online posts:** With careful planning, you can set up your social media posts for the entire week across all platforms. Social Jukebox and Hootsuite are my favorite sites for this. You take some time to organize your messaging on Sunday and set the frequency and times for when you want your posts to go live. It saves time and yields great results.

67. **Grocery bags:** If you can afford to print up some grocery bags, you can ask your local stores if you can donate those custom printed bags. I recommend that you ask the retailers first before spending any money on this one. They may not take third party solicitations. If they do, you will get into the homes of hundreds of people. Budget accordingly, though, as such bags can get really expensive, really fast.

68. **Drawing in public:** People always love to watch an artist in action. Bring out an oversized art pad and draw in public. Make sure that you do your best work, and be sure to have some business cards handy. For those people in the crowd that aren't afraid to come up to you, make sure you hand them a business card and remind them to check out your website.

69. **Permission walls:** Ask permission from store owners of local grocery stores or shops in a high traffic area that have their storefronts, walls or gates covered in graffiti. Offer to beautify their storefronts, walls or gates with one of your custom designs that will advertise both their brand and yours.

70. **Posters:** Create work that will make people want to take a picture of it and share it. Add a QR Code to the bottom corner that will connect the viewer to your website or social media site even faster. Posters can be hung up just about any place where people gather. You can

even ask trendy clothing and shoe stores if they will allow you to put up your work in their stores just to add to the décor of their store.

71. **Temporary tattoos:** Great idea when you're at an event: hire a street team or local students to wear a temporary tattoo with your logo or design. You can print these up at places like stickeryou.com. Great for free handouts as well. If you have a bit more money, you can hire a henna artist to mark everyone up.

72. **Self-publish a book:** Have a great idea for a book? Write it down and self-publish it. If you have valuable information or industry tips, you may be sitting on a gold mine. Setting yourself up as an expert, sets you apart from others in your industry. Publishing a book could also open you up for speaking opportunities as well as merchandise sales.

73. **Group art show:** Get a group of your art friends together, rent a local gallery, and have your own art show. As a group, you will be able to bring in more guests and new potential clients. Make sure, however, that everyone has a different niche so that everyone is unique.

74. **Partner with local library:** Libraries pride themselves on community engagement. Offer to host an art workshop for kids or adults. If it's free, they will be all ears! Such a workshop will give their patrons reasons to come back to library and may land you new followers or clients.

75. **Create an afterschool program:** This can be a lengthy process, but can be very rewarding once you sign all the paperwork. If your target market is children, you will be establishing a relationship with the school that has access to hundreds of children.

76. **Paid Instagram/Facebook ads:** This tip can be a bit expensive. I have had a bigger return on my investment by running Instagram ads than Facebook ads. However, that's just my experience. The reality: if no one is aware that you exist, you will have a harder time getting noticed. What I like to do is post an unpaid ad and see how well it performs. If the ad gets high engagement, likes, or comments, then I

pay for that post to be advertised. No sense paying for a post that no one is engaging with.

77. **Barter your services:** Businesses exchanging services is a fantastic concept. Make sure that both of you are walking away happy with this deal.

78. **Donate Clothing:** Donate branded clothing or other materials with your illustrations or logo on it to local non-profits. Shelters can always use sweaters for the population that they serve.

79. **Record a podcast:** Share your brand's story. Remember, facts tell, stories sell. Podcasts can enable you to reach new markets. This is a low-cost way to spread the word, but you'll need to do some research on how best to reach those new markets.

80. **Media interviews:** Request to be interviewed by online news sites, media companies, and local newspapers. Create a compelling reason for the coverage. Is it impactful? Are you offering a unique event or service? Once you are able to get one interview, you can use it as leverage to get more publicity.

81. **Write a press release:** While this tip may not be the cheapest item in this list, a well written press release can spread around among online media, newspaper and blog sites relatively quickly. The press release of course needs to be newsworthy. A new event, workshop, product or incredible service may be your newsworthy item for the press release. PRnewswire and PRWeb are two of the biggest press release services out there.

82. **Comic strips:** Create industry-related comic strips that either share some knowledge in a humorous way or poke fun at your industry. Posting such comic strips on social media can help to share it with other people in your industry.

83. **Live stream:** Set up a camera in your workspace or use screen capture video programs to record as you draw. Everyone loves to see the process. It's entertaining and you can use it as an opportunity to engage online with your followers.

84. **Recycle your content:** Your content may be old to you, but it's new to the new followers and contacts that you've made since you lasted

posted it. Repost and repurpose your content. Chop up your live stream video into 30 second tutorials or turn online articles into an e-book. Recycling your work is a great way to stay in the public eye especially if it was good content in the first place.

85. **Local radio interviews:** Start in your community. Having local support is important. The community wants to highlight people who are positive role models.

86. **Enter film festivals often**: Obviously, you have to be an animator or filmmaker, but the films that are chosen are screened in front of large audiences, giving you maximum exposure. Keep in mind, however, that most film festivals require an entry fee. FilmFreeway.com has a huge list of festivals worth entering.

87. **24-hour sale:** This one creates a sense of urgency. No one wants to miss out on a great discount. Offer something unique, but be sure to build people up before you announce the sale. Then, give them a few days to prepare for the upcoming 24-hour sale.

88. **Crowdfunding:** In case you've lived in a cave the last few years, get familiar with the concept of "crowdfunding. This is a method of raising small amounts of money via various websites such as gofundme.com to support your campaign. The result: your campaign gets wide distribution and you gain new supporters while you create a new pipeline of revenue. Crowdfunding is also a great way to determine if your products are marketable.

89. **Create a press kit:** Prepare a great presentation about your business and skillsets to drop off to selected media for promotional use. The press kit can provide all kinds of promotional materials and sticker giveaways, but essentially provides information about you, your company and any previous media or article write ups on your company.

90. **Speaking engagements:** This is a great revenue stream once you get it going. Start by contacting universities and schools and offer to speak on topics that you are knowledgeable about and that are relevant to your products or services.

SPEAKING ENGAGEMENT

Scan this QR Code to view a clip from one of my speaking engagements.

91. **Hire a public relations (PR) person:** Richard Branson said it best: "A good PR story is infinitely more effective than a front-page ad." A PR expert can help you tell the right story. Their services aren't cheap, but they may have relationships with news outlets, magazines, and others in your industry already. Press elevates the perception of your brand and a professional PR person can help position you to get the right story out.

92. **Create a bizarre promotion:** The more your promotion stirs up audiences, the more attention it can get. Stay within your company brand and core values, but get creative with your wording. You want to get people talking about your business and you!

93. **Contact your local news:** Do you have a story worth telling? Are you giving back to the community? Create a compelling story and reach out to your local news outlets. Journalists are always looking for stories, so work to make sure they tell your story.

NEWS COVERAGE

Scan this QR Code to view a clip from a local news story on Heroes of Color.

94. **Volunteer for a charity event:** Be careful that you don't come off as bragging about your charity work. Be sincere and show that you are involved in your community.

95. **Donate Artwork:** If your work is child friendly, consider donating it to the children's waiting rooms at hospitals, shelters or schools.

96. **Customer loyalty:** Create an exclusive incentive or deal specifically for your current or previous clients. Done right, this will re-kindle the need for your services with old clients you haven't heard from for a while.

97. **Write articles on Linkedin.com:** Linkedin is literally swarming with professionals brandishing their academic achievements and accomplishments. Writing a good article can bring traffic to your website, and promote your products and services. Most importantly, publishing such an article creates the perception that you are an expert in a specific field or topic.

98. **Submit proposals:** Presenting ideas to organizations, museums, and large companies rather than just individuals, opens you up to larger paying projects, bigger opportunities and much more exposure. Make sure again that you are solving a problem for the organization and offering a unique solution to that problem. Even if they've used similar products or services, just add your own special spin to it.

99. **Attend conferences:** Once you have clearly identified who your target market is, start attending the conferences that the target market members go to. Conferences can expand your list of contacts and increase your chances of landing new clients.

100. **Partner with influencers:** A well-established business can do wonders to your business relatively quickly. Find a business whose products complement (not compete with) your products. Create a contest, event or campaign that is mutually beneficial to you both.

101. **Custom-painted apparel:** If you're an artist, create an amazing custom-painted set of clothes with a jean jacket, canvas sneakers, and a trucker cap. It will literally stop people in their tracks. If you're not an artist, hire someone to do this for you. It's a huge attention grabber!

Chapter Eight

HOW TO CREATE MULTIPLE REVENUE STREAMS

8 SIMPLE STRATEGIES TO GROW YOUR BUSINESS

The starving artist is a thing of the past! Your sustainability as a freelancer, though, depends on your ability to promote yourself and your work. Putting yourself out there doesn't just refer to marketing and brand awareness. If you're not consistently looking for ways to create new opportunities for yourself, you will always be that "starving artist."

Putting yourself and your company out there in the world also refers to you applying for temporary creative work, artist's grants, creative competitions, pitching proposals and so much more. Don't just hunt for work. Instead position yourself so that people are also hunting for you. To help you sustain your efforts here, I have – surprise! – created another list of marketing strategies. Some of these strategies originate with the original list of 101 killer marketing techniques from Chapter Seven but these are a bit more fleshed out.

The fact is that the more opportunities you seek, the better chance you will have of landing multiple freelance gigs. Here then are eight different strategies that you can use to grow your business by generating multiple revenue streams. As you read them, be prepared to take action. None of these tips will work unless you do:

1. **Read More Books:** Every freelance entrepreneur should have an active reading list. It's always interesting to learn what successful CEO's are reading, mostly because they can serve as a guide to help you with your own business. Whether it's fiction or non-fiction, reading helps stimulate your mind and sparks new ideas. Set a goal of creating a list of at least 40 books you want to read this year. Whatever your current business challenges are, you can bet that someone has already "been there and done that." Learn from their triumphs as well as their mistakes. Business sites like Entrepreneur, Forbes and The Harvard Business Review regularly contain lists that can help you grow your business.

2. **Virtual Agents:** The job of an agent is to help find their clients work. Virtual agents or freelance websites are the same idea. Instead of an actual agent trying to find you work opportunities, these amazing freelance websites do all of the gig hunting for you. On most of these sites, you have to set up your profile page, upload some portfolio items, and set parameters for the types of freelance work you are seeking.

   On other sites, you'll need to do a keyword search for specific design work you are seeking. Craigslist is a great example of this.

Searching through the category of creative gigs you will help you find multiple opportunities, both local and nationwide. The difference here is that you must have a website to link back to once you apply to any of the freelance opportunities.

It's not enough to just attach a few samples of your work. Having your own online portfolio opens you up to a global market. Also, important to note: setting up a profile page on most of these sites is free. There are some additional perks that are given to those who do pay for add-ons. But even with the basic, free subscription, you will be able to find some work. Once you set up your page, you will start receiving emails notifying you of freelance gigs that match your creative interests. While there are many similar sites that are in existence, here is my "list within a list" of some of the most profitable virtual agents that you should start using to search for freelance opportunities:

- Upwork.com
- guru.com
- freelancer.com
- craigslist.com
- sevendays.co (yes, it's .co, not .com)
- 99designs
- designcrowd.com
- toptal.com

Missing from this list are low revenue sites such as fiverr and fourerr – where you can find cheap services of just about any kind. While there are some freelancers who have had success on these sites, the key word to remember here is cheap. Do you really want the first word that people associate your products and services with to be cheap?

3. **Referral incentive program:** Before Facebook was the No. 1 social network on the planet, Myspace was the most visited

social networking site from 2005 - 2008. It seemed like everyone on Myspace was either a musician, DJ, or a rapper. This was where I met that good friend and longtime client, Mario "DJ Chonz" Rodriguez. He hired me to create a custom cartoon character for him. Since I knew he was part of a DJ crew which had several members, I presented him with a deal. If he got me three clients who paid me $500 or more, I would create a free custom design for him of equal value.

It didn't take long for him to get me well over six paid clients. I have since used the referral incentive program with other clients with equal success. Try to close the deal first and then offer it to them once they have become your client. They are more likely to help you, once you have established a working relationship with each other.

4. **Creative staffing agencies:** While you have your virtual agents working for you on the Internet, you can have staffing agencies working for you offline. The real big spenders are the staffing agencies. They have benefited immensely from freelancers. When I think about staffing agencies, I immediately think of being called on temp job assignments where you're asked to lick envelopes until your tongue blisters, fetch coffee or doing other mundane tasks.

   The difference between staffing agencies and creative staffing agencies is that creative staffing agencies specialize in finding you creative work only. I have been placed on freelance gigs working at DC Collectibles, Ogilvy & Mather, Havas Edge, and Warner Bros. Animation just to name a few. I was surprised to learn that often times the companies were even open to remote work. You can sign up with these agencies like any other job by filling out an online application, submitting your resume, and providing a link to your online portfolio. Once a recruiter gets a hold of your information, they will set up an interview based on the strength of your portfolio. After you've met in person and outlined your design objectives, the recruiter takes it from there.

MOTION GRAPHICS

Scan this QR Code to view a clip from a motion graphics clip I did at Havas Edge.

While there are several dozen reputable creative staffing agencies to choose from, I have listed my top five below. Please do your own research on other creative staffing agencies in your area. Our list:

- 24seventalent.com
- Creativecircle.com
- Aquent
- Artisan
- Randstadusa.com

5. **Create Merchandise:** With the rise of numerous POD (print on demand) companies out there, you no longer have to fear sitting on boxes of unsold merchandise. Creating merchandise is just half the battle. The other crucial half is developing a solid marketing plan on how you intend to sell your products.

   In 2006, after I quit my job at Walt Disney Feature Animation, I decided to create a new line of T-shirts specifically designed for Dominican people who lived in New York City. I didn't know much about POD's back then, so I went to a traditional silk screen printer. I started with one t-shirt design that only had one color. I sold the shirts for $10 online and sold well over 300 shirts with ease. With my confidence boosted, I felt I could take it to the next level and create additional Dominican T-shirt designs and start selling them at events in Los Angeles.

   This turned out to be a very expensive mistake. I failed to research the demographic of the events that I was attending. Yes, I had lots of new merchandise, but no one related to the designs. People who approached my table at events didn't even know what a "Dominican" was. I spent close to $3,000 on new shirts and had boxes of merchandise sitting in my closet for the rest of that year. I'm all about taking calculated risks, but you have to plan your approach, and the numbers have to make sense.

The downside to the POD's is that they take a pretty sizable profit margin from your sales. Rates vary widely from company to company, and even from product to product. As an example, I recently created an amazing hoodie sweatshirt design that I wanted to sell. I marked the sweater at $40 retail price. Once the item sold, the company that I used (teespring.com) handled everything from printing to shipping. All I had to do was upload my artwork to the shirt. Their cut from the sweater was about $19.75, leaving me with a $20.25 profit. Not bad considering that I spent no money to produce any of the shirts, and won't have to worry about sitting on merchandise if I don't sell it.

I've learned that there are some pros and cons to POD's, some of which mean that I won't use them for every creative merchandise item I create. Using POD's for creating t-shirt merchandise is, however, great for online sales, but if you're at a live event, you might want to consider going to a traditional silk screen printer.

6. **Apply for Artist's Grants**: You don't necessarily have to be a grant writer to get an artist's grant, but it helps. Surprisingly, there are some visual artist's grants out there for us that we qualify for and the application process isn't all that difficult. Know your project well, and carefully research the different foundations offering such grants. Then, get familiar with the types of projects they fund. If they are funding community murals but you're a graphic designer, then that's obviously not the right fit.

    The Artwork Archive has an incredible list of artist's grants with direct links to the individual grants. In fact, there are way too many to list. The following link will help you find well over 100 artist's grants including those for digital artists, fine artists, photographers, sculptors, graphic designers and much more. Go to www.artworkarchive.com/blog and type in the keyword "grants" in the search box. Multiple articles will pop up, including a complete guide to artist grant opportunities.

Note, however, that you have to be very mindful of their funding cycles. Very few foundations offer rolling applications. There is usually a deadline that you are given to submit all of your materials. Foundations usually only award grants once or twice a year. Apply today, and keep moving forward.

7. **Constantly make proposals:** This particular idea has changed the trajectory of my business. I have learned to focus more on pitching ideas, events and workshops to businesses, schools and organizations. The money is better, and you can make a larger impact. Not only that, landing these gigs can really help set you up as a leading authority in your speciality. The key is finding organizations that align with your values and design services. Make it a habit to pitch to at least one to two new design proposals a month to organizations that you feel would benefit from your services. Remember to first learn as much as you can about the company to which you are pitching before you actually make a pitch. Sell them on the benefits they receive by using your services – re-review my discussion of "problem/solution" steps in Chapter Seven of this book.

8. **Crowdfunding:** There are some obvious perks to launching a crowdfunding campaign. Aside from the money you raise, you may also find out who your supporters really are. Crowdfunding is also a great way to check to see if there is a current interest in the projects or products that you create. While some of your supporters might be friends and family, you should also gain new followers who just want to learn about your company and are attracted by your company's mission. Being a freelancer isn't just about offering services for others, but also includes building projects of your own. You don't need to launch a $20,000 campaign - start small and learn all of the elements involved in crowdfunding and building an organic email list in the process.

EXERCISE #6 - BUSINESS STRATEGIES

Create your own reading list: Make a list of at least 40 books that you would like to read by the end of the year. Check online for ideas of what other entrepreneurs are reading. Picking books on business, start-ups, freelancing, and fiction are all good choices.

Set up your account: Pick at least 3 virtual agent sites, sign up, and set up your online portfolio. Make it a habit to search for gigs related to your design expertise.

Create an account: Sign up with 24seventalent, randstadusa and creativecircle if you are a designer, illustrator, animator, editor or other creative. They can help place you at some amazing companies which specifically seek creatives.

For Sale – Your Merchandise: Create one piece of merchandise that you can put your designs on and post it on your website for sale. Advertise it on all your social media pages.

Search for a grant: Log on to www.artworkarchive.com/blog and search for upcoming grants that you might be qualified for. Getting into the practice of applying for grants – it's a great habit. Aside from potentially being awarded a grant, it tightens up your pitch and helps you describe your products and services a lot better.

EXHIBITING: TRADESHOW SECRETS

All artists who specialize in cartooning, illustration, animation, graphic design, or comic book design should exhibit as a vendor at trade shows. Look for ones that are relevant to your industry of course, but don't miss out on the comic-cons across the nation. There are several reasons to consider exhibiting at the major comic-con tradeshows like the ones in San Diego or New York.

One of the biggest advantages is that you have an opportunity to test your product on the spot. You get to see first-hand if the products that you're creating generate interest. You can test out new products and get real-time feedback from your customers.

Exhibiting also gives you an opportunity to test your pricing. You have the flexibility to change it according to how people react to your prices. Exhibiting can give your brand much needed visibility while allowing you to earn money and network with other professionals in your industry. Before you run off and start signing up for tradeshows, however, here are a few tradeshow secrets you should consider.

- **Show attendance:** How many people attend this tradeshow? Nothing wrong with attending, smaller more intimate tradeshows, but don't waste time on small shows where you end up spending more than you make. Get the biggest bang for your buck and go where the action is.
- **Cost effective:** Think about how much it costs to register for the event (free is good!), travel to an out-of-town event, print up merchandise, hotels, food, etc. It can get expensive. Make sure that you are giving yourself a chance to earn that money back. A three-day event will give you the best chance to work the crowd and get you a reasonable return on your investment.
- **Payment options:** Make this an easy experience for the customer. If they don't have cash, no problem. With multiple payment options available like Venmo, Paypal, and Square, there should be no reason why you can't handle non-cash payments. Another obstacle to plan for is the lack of Wifi or a bad connection at the exhibition. Lack of connectivity obviously makes it difficult to handle electronic payments. Ask the event organizer about the available Wifi ahead of time. Consider activating your phone's hotspot and essentially using your own Wifi. Oh, and make sure your phone is charged! Don't leave that to chance – there's no reason to lose a sale because your phone died.
- **Signs and Banners:** Make it easy for people to find you. Create some dazzling banners, signs, or even tablecloths if you have the

money for it. Standing out can be hard to do when you're jam packed next to other exhibitors. Your vibrant banner display is the best way to get people to your table without even opening your mouth.

- **Have you attended a trade show before?** The best strategy for any exhibitor is to attend the event as an attendee first. Get a feel for the products people sell, the crowd, their spending habits, their age bracket, etc. Speak to some of the exhibitors, ask them about their experiences at the show. Before you make an investment, you want to get a feel for the crowd so that you can create products that they want.

- **Promotional materials:** One of the most crucial steps in exhibiting is ensuring that you have enough promotional materials to hand out. Even if people are not able to get to your table, having well designed promotional material will increase your chances of website visits that may convert into sales.

- **Create affordable products:** Create products that aren't expensive to make yet yield high profit margins. Art prints are a great example of this. You can get 11x17, full color art prints for 75¢ and sell them for $10. Live sketches are also great. You buy an art pad for $10 with 50 pages. If you sell 50 sketches for $10 you made a quick $500.

- **Dress to impress:** Not really "impress," but you definitely want to stand out from the rest of the exhibitors. Your brand doesn't only include the design of your booth, products, and signage. Most importantly, your brand is you! Dress up as one of your characters, or wear clothing that ensures that people will stop and look. The objective is to attract attention so you can sell your products and services.

- **Keep your head up:** I don't mean that as an inspirational phrase, I mean literally, keep your head up! Make eye contact with everyone who looks in your direction, otherwise the vendor right next to you will engage with your clients and take your sales. Unless you're doing a commissioned sketch, save the drawing for another time.

- **Actively engage with customers:** People buy from people they like. Even if people don't stop by your table, smile and say hello to people. When you come off as a genuine likable person you have a higher chance of selling your products.

- **Just passing by:** Don't let anyone walk past your table without handing them branded, promotional material. Sometimes they will throw it away. At other times they will put it in their goodie bag. There will, however, be some people who will stop, turn around and walk back to your table. Give your friends some flyers and have them walk around and hand flyers out to people. Ask if this is okay because some conventions don't allow you to hand out promotional materials. To counter this, strategically drop some of your flyers on the floor at specific locations where groups of people sit or stand in line. Restroom and cafeteria areas are good spots.

- **Fake crowds:** You're not always going to have a lot of traffic at your table. One trick is to invite about 10 friends to join you at the event. If there are crowds forming, but no one is coming to your table, ask your friends to crowd around your table. It creates the perception that your table is worth checking out. As onlookers start trickling in, your friends can start backing out from the crowd one by one to make room for the actual customers.

- **Deals and discounts:** Everyone loves a deal. Play around with your pricing by offering "Buy one, get one free" or other sales tactics to get people interested in purchasing from you. Figure out other deals and ways to engage people and bring them to your table.

10 TYPES OF TRADESHOW CUSTOMERS

Despite what you have been told, you cannot treat all clients the same. Some will require more patience, but still others you must cut off before they talk your ears off. You never know who you will meet when you are exhibiting at an event, so it's important to recognize some different personality types. These are some of the most common personality types that you can expect to visit your exhibition table:

1. **The Rambler:** This is the person who just can't stop talking. They speak about random things that have nothing to do with you or your products. They attempt to have these long drawn out conversations with you while you're trying work your table. Be polite, but let the Rambler know that you have to excuse them so that you can handle the next client. Be very mindful of how you treat them. Other people will be watching you so if handle it poorly, it will negatively affect your business. One idea is that you can turn the Rambler into an assistant of some sort. Give them a task to help you. Give them some flyers and ask them to help you distribute flyers. Use their energy to your advantage.

2. **The Browser:** No matter how great your products are, there will always be people who stop by just to look. They may look through all of your merchandise, hold it in their hands, smile and compliment you, but in the end, they don't buy anything. Don't take it personally even if you did all of the right things to engage with them and they simply walk off. It's not a reflection of your work - they have already made up their mind that they have no intention of taking their wallet out to buy something.

3. **The Instant Buyer:** These of course are your best customers. They come straight up to your table, see what they want, and buy it. If you're fortunate enough to get some of these customers, be sure to get their contact information. If they liked your work that much, they will not hesitate to buy from you again.

4. **The Hater:** These are just miserable people who want you to be miserable, too. Don't expend any energy on them. If you do, they will just suck the positive energy from you and that's the last thing you need at a trade show. Exhibiting at major events requires a lot

of effort, so keep your energy level up. You can't afford to spend time on people who aren't happy for you.

5. **The Bargain Shopper:** These people are always searching for a deal. They want everything at a discounted rate. They will try to talk you down from your set prices. You can be flexible with them if it makes sense. For example, bundle up some merchandise such as "buy three, get one free" or something like that. Value your work and don't feel obliged to keep bringing the price down just because someone fails to see the value in that work.

6. **The Cheapskate:** They're very similar to the bargain shopper, but the big difference is after the negotiating, the bargain shopper actually buys something from you. The cheapskate would rather not spend any money if they don't have to. They also like to complain that everything you have is too expensive.

7. **The Life Story Talker:** It isn't about you, it's all about them. They will fill your ear with personal details of their life that you don't need to hear. You have to extinguish these conversations quickly as they could be a major turn off for other potential clients who are standing by your table. If somebody is trying to make a purchase or has a quick question, you have to politely excuse the life story talker.

8. **The Follower:** The Follower is inspired when they see others buying your products. These are great customers because they are easily convinced.

9. **Customer Requests:** When customers love your work so much, they may request custom designs. These commissioned projects will be priced way more than anything you have on your exhibition table. While they are still emotionally hooked on your work, collect their information and try to negotiate a deposit on the spot before their impulsiveness wears off.

10. **The Raving Fan:** Raving Fans are the ones that have been watching you or following you online. They regularly engage with all of your social media posts. These become repeat customers, advocates, and can be your biggest supporters.

EXPECT THE UNEXPECTED

Expect that things will go wrong during your exhibition. While you can't plan for every mishap, your ability to bounce back from obstacles will determine how successful your show will be. Recently, I attended an outdoor art exhibition in a park in Santa Clarita, California. It was a beautiful show full of dozens of talented painters, artists, illustrators, authors and craft makers.

One lady had an amazing display. It was elaborate and cleverly designed to grab people's attention. As groups of people flocked over to her table, I noticed the winds were a bit stronger than usual. Seconds later, the wind blasted her signs and toppled over her entire display, banner, business cards, merchandise - everything. Her exhibit was totally ruined.

The poor woman never recovered. She spent the rest of her time trying to set up again and again and again. Just when she thought she had it right, the wind reminded her who was boss. Other exhibitors met a similar fate, but they were able to bounce back by quickly changing their displays in a way that the wind would not affect them. Those who bounced back adopted to their environment and continued to make sales. Those who didn't adapt well will probably think twice before doing another outdoor show. Whether you exhibit indoors or outdoors, have a back-up plan you can immediately deploy.

TOP COMIC CON TRADESHOWS FOR ARTISTS

Comic conventions ("Comic Cons") across the nation have exploded in popularity. They're not just for comic book creators. Other industries have carved their niche into the comic book world, too, such as fashion, music, fine artists, animation, toys, collectibles, etc.

LIST OF 100 TOP TRADESHOWS

Scan this QR Code to view an extensive list of the top 100 comic conventions.

As of this writing, here are the top 15 conventions for illustrators:

1. Anime Expo (Los Angeles)
2. San Diego Comic Con
3. New York Comic Con
4. Emerald City Comic Con (Seattle)
5. Wondercon (Los Angeles)
6. Heroes Con (Charlotte)
7. Chicago Comic and Entertainment Expo
8. Megacon (Orlando)
9. Salt Lake City Comic Con
10. Comikaze Expo
11. Wizard World (Philadelphia)
12. Otakon (Washington D.C.)
13. Fan Expo (Canada)
14. Denver Pop Culture Con (Denver Comic Con)
15. Dragon Con (Atlanta)

YOU MUST BELIEVE IT TO ACHIEVE IT!

DON'T JUST DEFINE YOUR PURPOSE, LIVE IT.

As freelance artists, we tend to grab any opportunity that comes our way. As you build your reputation, it is important to give some serious thought as to what your purpose as a designer really is. Knowing this purpose will help align you to jobs that fit your personal values. I have always described my purpose to be the promotion of inclusion and diversity by educating through art and animation. During a trip to a toy vault at DC Collectibles, I learned that my purpose was more than just a mission statement or cool tag line. It was in fact the code by which I live by every day.

It happened on my last day working at DC Collectibles in the summer of 2018. My supervisor knew that I had three small children, and was kind enough to send me off with some gifts for them. We walked into this huge vault and he said, take whatever you want! As amazing as it sounded, I found myself searching for several minutes before I actually grabbed at anything that interested me. All I kept thinking was wow, look at all these white, male heroes.

I worried that, subconsciously, I was doing little to combat the lack of positive representation of people of color by bringing my kids some white heroes instead of more ethnically diverse options. Maybe I was overthinking this a bit, but the lack of diversity in the vault was clearly evident. I searched for merchandise with ethnic heroes and I only found three.

Though I walked away from the vault with very little, I learned a lot about myself. Society creates labels for us but they don't get to define who you are. That's your choice. You get to define who you are through your actions, values and beliefs. When you live a life of purpose, your values will influence the decisions that you make, even something as trivial as selecting toys with brown skin for your kids to play with. When I arrived home that day and handed my kids their toys, I saw them light up inside. They were able to identify with the characters. My choices made it easy for them to imagine themselves as superpowered heroes because they identified with toys that looked like they did.

STEP OUT OF YOUR COMFORT ZONE

One of the most difficult challenges we face in our lives is to willingly deviate from the norm. Artists don't always adapt very well to change. When we find a medium, style or method that works for us, we stay loyal to it. Back in 2004, when I worked at Walt Disney Feature Animation, I remembered a coworker telling me that many of the legendary artists and animators were let go because many of them were not able to transition to digital drawing and 3D animation. Making a change requires a lot of courage to step out of your comfort zone, and into a new world that you don't feel comfortable with or confident in. Understand, however, that your future as a freelancer depends on your ability to adapt. The amazing thing is, that's when growth happens. You learn new skills and tactics, and even your outlook changes.

In June 2019, I was forced to step out of my comfort zone when Scholastic invited me to attend the American Library Association conference in Washington, D.C. It was a three-day event not dissimilar to that of the San Diego Comic Convention. The second day of the event, three other authors and I were invited to give five-minute speeches about the type of impact we hoped our books would make in the community. Speaking on the stage to a packed crowd was the easy part, but what followed was the challenge.

It wasn't the fact that I sat next to an award-winning author at our book signing, and it wasn't that I was sitting at a book signing event with no books to sign (just posters due to a last-minute art changes). What bothered me was that I was totally ignored while I watched an adoring public salivating over the author sitting next to me - that was uncomfortable!

Admittedly I had never been to a book signing and did not know what to expect or how I should react. I could have been depressed by the situation, but I didn't. Instead of hating on the popular author for drawing a fanatical following to his side of the table, I turned this situation into a teaching moment.

As I saw how he warmed the crowd, smiled at them, and just made the fans feel so important, I took notes. Since everyone had badges, he spoke their names, and gave everyone eye contact. For me, school was definitely in session and I had the front row seat! Regardless of the circumstances, chances are you will be faced with an uncomfortable situation in your career. When it arrives, handle it head on and take the opportunity to learn from it.

AMERICAN LIBRARY ASSOCIATION

Scan this QR Code to view a clip from my ALA event with Scholastic.

STAY RELEVANT

There is nothing more frightening for a freelance artist than to know that their skillsets have become obsolete. If you're a digital artist, this can happen rather quickly as technology constantly changes at such a rapid rate. The struggle to remain relevant isn't as difficult as one might think. There are so many free resources available to us thanks to the internet. Here are a few quick suggestions on how to boost your skillsets:

- **Tutorials:** While going back to school seems like the obvious option, the internet has done some heavy lifting for freelancers. The quickest, cheapest and easiest way to upgrade your skillset is by watching tutorials on websites like Lynda, Udemy, YouTube and other sites that have hundreds of videos pertaining to the latest design software. Most tutorials will be available to you for free.

- **Webinars:** Another remote classroom option. Live webinars are great because they give you an opportunity to get real-time feedback from the instructors hosting the webinar. Webinars are also often available free of charge.

- **Conferences:** Keep an eye out for industry-related events. They are usually packed with influential guest speakers and often hold some amazing, hands on workshops. It's a great way to network and see what some of the experts in your field are up to. While you may have to pay to attend, conferences can be a great tool for learning and making new contacts with people in your industry.

- **Workshops:** The Small Business Administration (SBA) hosts a series of often free webinars and workshops. Though they are not usually art related, remember that art is a business and you must expand your business savvy in order to manage your art career successfully.

- **College Courses:** Sign up for some continuing education classes at your local community college or prestigious private art college. This is a great way to keep your pulse on the art world. You learn not just from your instructor but from students as well.

- **Your Network:** You should surround yourself with freelancers who are just killin' the game. If you don't know any, search some groups on social media. Look at the industry conferences in your genre – who are the guest speakers, panellists, and exhibitors? Make a friend a day and you'll keep growing that way!

Educating yourself is not just a great investment in yourself, but also in your business. Remember: the learning never stops and as technology continues to advance, you can always find new ways to entice new clients but most importantly, keep existing clients coming back. Freelancers who do not modify their skills run the risk of becoming extinct!

Go online and watch one new tutorial a week on a subject that you love or on an entirely new creative program or technique. Take a refresher course or learn something new. Challenge yourself to keep finding ways to grow. The idea is that you want to make it a habit to keep learning new material and stay relevant with technology applicable to your industry.

CREATE OPPORTUNITIES

There is no doubt that as you navigate this freelance journey, you will be offered some amazing opportunities. Sometimes, opportunities will stare you right in your face but, because you have not taken the time to reflect on who you are and what you have to offer, the opportunity will slip right through your fingers. To recognize an opportunity, you must be able to identify not just the services that you can offer, but also your ability to recognize your strengths, talents, values, objectives, resources, and confidence in yourself.

Once you have identified what you can bring to the table, you will be better prepared to start honing in on opportunities that are uniquely suited to meet your company goals and objectives. As I discussed in Chapter Three, my story of how I landed my Scholastic book deal by sneaking into a poetry workshop is an incredible example of how I created an opportunity for myself. When Deb Dugan asked me if I was working on creating a children's book and I saw the doors of opportunity opening up, I quickly asked myself these questions before answering "yes":

1. Am I capable of creating a children's book? Yup.
2. Do I have the software needed? Absolutely.
3. Can I write and illustrate it myself? I sure can!
4. Can I submit a manuscript with art in 7 days or less? I'd need lots of coffee, but yes.
5. Have I ever self-published a book before? No, but I'll read some books and learn!

When you recognize a potential opportunity, you must be ready to pounce on it! It can happen in the blink of an eye, but when you know what you want, opportunities that align with your objectives will become easier to spot.

RECOGNIZE OPPORTUNITY AND SEIZE IT!

Spotting an opportunity and quickly assessing your ability to take that project on is a decision that you might be forced to make in a split second. When you believe in yourself, this confidence is what allows you to make those lightning fast decisions.

But what happens when you're not 100% sure of yourself? What if you take too long to answer to an opportunity of a lifetime? In that situation, heed the advice of Sir Richard Branson: "If somebody offers you an amazing opportunity but you are not sure you can do it, say yes, then learn how to do it later."

The minute you show a client an ounce of doubt, you will assuredly lose them. This almost happened to me in 2011 when I landed the largest client in my career. The client was Pearson, the global leaders in education. What started as a simple 60-second animation gig that I was commissioned to do off of Craigslist turned into my first office space with 10 freelance artists working for me. Prior to this I always worked from home.

After the Pearson job was completed, the client told me that his boss wanted to meet me. I didn't think anything of it. I showed up to this meeting in downtown Los Angeles, and the three of us met casually as we walked into an executive suite board room. There were suits all around the room. There I was standing with shorts, t-shirt and a hat to the back. I was not prepared for this, I thought to myself.

Getting right to business, Larry, the project manager, quickly briefed me on what the project entailed. They needed over 200 animated videos ranging from one to two minutes in length. Oh yea, and they needed all 200 animated videos delivered in 12 months! He looked at me and said, "Do you have the bandwidth to handle this job? If so, how soon can you and your team get started on it?"

All of a sudden, I felt so unsure of myself and my abilities. I knew this was going to be a big job, and I didn't have a team. I was working from home, and only owned one outdated laptop that was severely paralyzed. But, how could I pass up an opportunity of a lifetime?

Without knowing how I would complete the job, hire a crew, get an office and staff up immediately, I turned to Larry and responded, "Larry, we are ready to hit the ground running. We can get started as soon as you're able to pay my 50% deposit." He smiled and said, "great, send me the invoice and let's get rolling." No questions asked. We shook hands and in less than five minutes, I was out the door.

My chest was tight, my head hurt, I was sweaty and my knees felt weak. Did I really just secure a six-figure job in five minutes? Yup. Actually, the contract ended up lasting three years because we were commissioned to create videos explaining the common core math and reading standards. Working for two different departments at Pearson was a lot of fun. It was the first time in my life that I earned a six-figure salary doing what I loved and on my terms.

Part of my crew of animators, inkers, and storyboard artists.

That brief client meeting with Pearson taught me that you don't have to have all of the answers all the time. You don't need to be the most skilled worker, just a resourceful one. Most importantly, you have to believe in yourself so much that it makes others believe in you. Larry believed in me because I believed in myself. We are all taught to follow the leader. When you know yourself and speak confidently, you set yourself up as an expert and therefore you become a leader.

CONVINCE YOURSELF, NOT YOUR CLIENTS

In art school, you are surrounded by talented faculty, staff and students. When I started at the School of Visual Arts, I was actually very intimidated my first year because I felt like everyone had more talent than I did. Even though I was just as talented, I had little confidence in my own skills. What I didn't realize was that this was the perfect environment to foster creativity and growth.

Once I allowed myself to be inspired and not intimidated, I saw tremendous growth in my art skills. I started hanging out with all the top students and soaked up as much knowledge as I could. That boosted my confidence and I slowly started to convince myself that I was equally as talented as my colleagues.

In the same way that you feed off negative energy, you feed off the positive. Keep surrounding yourself with amazing people and you will learn some of their amazing habits. As Albert Einstein said, **"Stay away from negative people, they have a problem for every solution."**

The freelancing landscape isn't much different from the collegiate one. There is also a bit of friendly competition that exists among freelancers. On the other hand, not all freelance jobs go to the most skilled or talented. Having connections, being at the right place at the right time, or sometimes just having the confidence needed to win a client's trust will increase your success rate. Whatever the reason, when that opportunity arrives, you must be ready to pounce on the opportunity.

In the year 2000, I was a second-year animation student at the School of Visual Arts. I was working as an intern at a small animation studio.

131

There was this intern who was a phenomenal animator who was also a second-year animation student. She was exceptional in everything she did and when the owner of the studio got calls for freelance gigs, he would often throw them her way.

One day, the owner handed her a job that she could not handle. He handed her the phone and within seconds she looked around the room as if she were looking for someone to save her. She looked at me, and quietly whispered, "Do you know Adobe After Effects?" I was familiar with the program, but I was no expert. I said "yes" and with that she handed me the phone!

I spoke to the client for about five minutes and ended up securing the freelance gig. The client was the New York City Lotto. It was just five seconds of animation, but it paid well and it was my first commercial animation gig. Two weeks later, it aired on television. I was not as skilled as my fellow intern was at the time but, in the end, it was my confidence that sold the client, not my work.

As freelancers it's expected that we should work towards convincing clients that we're the best person for the job. But what you must understand is that you first have to convince yourself that you're the right person for the job. You may have heard the expression, "fake it 'till you make it." That is horrible advice! When you fake anything, you're not being real with yourself. A better approach is to identify what your talents and your gifts are first. This way you will know what you are capable of handling. Be honest with yourself. Take the time to identify your strengths and your weaknesses.

THE JACK OF ALL TRADES AND MASTER OF NONE

We're often discouraged from becoming a jack of all trades and master of none. It makes sense. There are many different skills required to, for example, create an animated cartoon including writing, storyboarding, character design, layout, visual development, and the list goes on and on. As an animation student, you are taught each skill required to create an animated cartoon. The purpose of this is to hopefully help you find your strengths and master that one skill to perfection. When you work for someone else, this is key.

When you're a freelance artist, though, this is suicide! I can count well over a dozen times that being a jack of all trades has allowed me to upsell my clients resulting in bigger paying gigs just because I had multiple skillsets. Most artists have multiple disciplines that they can monetize. When you're a jack of all trades, you increase your chances of landing more freelance gigs.

Even if you're not skilled in multiple disciplines you can still profit off of others who are. Build a network of exceptional artists, and hire them to complete jobs that you don't have the time or skill to complete. Sometimes the easiest way to make money as a freelancer is to hire someone else to do it at a cheaper cost or, as the IT industry calls it, "outsource."

In 2011, I applied to a freelance job which was onsite at The South Bay Center for Counseling. The program was called "The Urban Art Center," and they were hiring a part-time art instructor assistant. The prescribed duties were to assist the urban arts instructor who was tasked with teaching students between the ages of 17-21 how to legally monetize their graffiti skills.

Street Bombing - New York City, Railroad tracks 1994.

133

Even though I used to be a graffiti writer back in high school, I was better on paper than I was on the wall. Still, I knew that my professional art background would serve as a selling point and potentially land me the position. What helped me was the years of exhibiting at tradeshows. I was able to use my graffiti skills to create custom hats, sneakers, and other merchandise and sell it. This was literally the mission of the organization. Needless to say, I made sure that my portfolio emphasized that background over my actual graffiti skills.

In addition to my art skills, the Center immediately recognized my genuine desire to help foster the talents of student artists. During the interview, I went on to pitch a series of ideas, workshops, and events and was hired on the spot. But wait: I wasn't hired as the assistant; I was hired as the lead Urban Arts Instructor! I developed a 12-week fine arts curriculum for all 70 students as well as an eight-week Photoshop class for a smaller group of about 12 students.

Along with these classes, I also developed the Center's promotional and marketing materials for events. It is not an exaggeration to say that my classes were the favorite among the students. Their attendance was never so high. A typical class was made up of 70 students and attendance never fell below 60.

By refocusing the Center's attention on my other skillsets, I became an integral part of the program. I went on to create and manage the Center's e-commerce website that was used to sell artwork created by the students for their end-of-the-year art show. Even though technically I wasn't the most skilled graffiti artist out there, I was able to get the Center to recognize my other talents and how they aligned with the Center's mission. I sold myself by selling to them the many benefits they would have by hiring me. This is the approach you want to take with your clients. You want them to know that you are exactly what they have been waiting for.

Chapter Ten

DELIVERING A SUCCESSFUL PITCH

PHOTO COURTESY OF BLACK PUBLIC MEDIA © COPYRIGHT 2019

DEVELOPING YOUR PITCH

Creating a successful design proposal is very similar to pitching a successful film project. While this chapter is pitched (pun intended) to animators and filmmakers, most of the principles I describe below can equally apply to your design pitches.

The first thing to remember: in order to give a good pitch, you need to have a product that's worth pitching. That seems obvious, but think about how compelling your film project might be. Your film or series has probably been done before so why should anyone care? In her 2018 article "The Art of the Elevator Pitch" in the Harvard Business Review, Carmine Gallo notes that "Hollywood screenwriters typically get three to five minutes to propose an idea, but it takes around 45 seconds for producers to know if they want to invest."

45 seconds! Obviously, you need to grab your audience's attention quickly with a strong opening and take them on a journey, but keep them hoping for more. Pitching is definitely a skill that is learned. Some people know how to work a crowd, some people don't. But the good news is that, with practice, anyone can learn this skill.

To make an impact on an audience or a group of executives, it helps to establish a connection with them. Discover your own personal narrative before you walk into the room. Think about how you define yourself as an individual. How does this define the stories that you tell? How does your personal narrative fuel the essence of your work?

Pitching is about how well you can transfer your positive energy to the people in the room. When you believe that this is your moment, you will own that pitch. Remember that people are interested in you before they get interested in your project. My brother Willy is a natural born hustler and a fantastic salesman. He has always told me, "It's not about your product, it's all about your pitch." While what you say is important, how you say it can make all the difference in the world.

EXERCISE #8 - CREATE YOUR ELEVATOR PITCH

Identify a problem, solution and proof of how your service or product will solve a problem. Use the example above as a guide. Pitch your service or product to a friend or family member and see if you can do it in 90 seconds. Time yourself! This will also help you in crafting your offer.

TAGLINES & LOGLINES

In order to influence people, you need to deliver your pitch in a memorable and exciting way. You're not just selling your product, you're selling yourself, your promotional material and anyone associated with your film. Create memorable moments for your audience. Then, identify one thing that you want your audience to remember. This is where taglines, loglines, and catch phrases are born.

Taglines are typically short one-liners used as marketing copy designed to go on posters and advertisements to promote or sell the film. These can be funny, very catchy and often very clever one-line descriptions of the movie. Here are some examples of taglines from major motion pictures that you might see on marketing materials:

- There are 3.7 trillion fish in the ocean. They're looking for one. (Finding Nemo)
- Just because they serve you doesn't mean they like you. (Clerks)
- One dream. Four Jamaicans. Twenty below zero. (Cool Runnings)

Loglines are longer, up to two sentences, that present a basic description of your plot in about 25 to 30 words. The logline should contain all the necessary elements of your story. Your goal is to create a storytelling experience that helps your audience remember and easily repeat your pitch to someone else. The most powerful loglines will identify the key elements of the story, the main character, their weaknesses, and the conflict and hurdles they need to overcome. Here are some examples of loglines from major motion pictures:

- During the U.S.-Vietnam War, Captain Willard is sent on a dangerous mission into Cambodia to assassinate a renegade colonel who has set himself up as a god among a local tribe. (Apocalypse Now)

- Forrest Gump, while not intelligent, has accidentally been present at many historic moments, but his true love, Jenny Curran, eludes him. (Forrest Gump)
- A young FBI cadet must confide in an incarcerated and manipulative killer to obtain his help on catching another serial killer who skins his victims. (Silence of The Lambs)

You can probably guess all three of these movies even if I hadn't posted the titles of the films. The key takeaway here is not to focus on the details of the movie. Instead the logline is just supposed to be an explanation of the conflict at the heart of the story. The logline should be easy to say and easy to remember

CONTENT, CONTEXT & FRAMING

Your pitches should be powered by content and leveraged by emotions. You should have a basic understanding of the content, context and framing of your pitch.

- **Content:** The actual pitch. This is what you must pitch in an emotional, powerful and concise manner that conveys it's artistic and commercial potential.
- **Context:** The emotion. The emotions inherent in the project, yourself and your belief in the project. This is what drives you to tell the story.
- **Framing:** The perspective. The wants, needs, pains, and fears of the buyer themselves. They want the hot project so convince them that you will bring the heat. Address any concerns they have. By alleviating their worries, your project becomes more appealing, because it's solving a problem.

30 TIPS TO A WINNING PITCH SESSION

Fear of public speaking is a very common phobia, and one that is believed to affect up to 75% of the population. If you have a fear of public speaking, I would highly recommend taking some workshops on how to pitch. Having great content means nothing if you don't know how to explain it. Practice helps ease the anxiety.

Surprisingly, exposing your nervousness to your audience or an executive can work in your favor. Don't try to hide it. Instead announce to your audience that this is the moment you have worked so hard for - to get this material in front of them. By exposing your fears, you will evoke emotions from your audience. Emotional connections are crucial to keeping audiences engaged. After disclosing your fears, your audience will be on your side. When you come off as a genuine, likeable person, people will be on your side because they want you to succeed. Here are 30 great tips to help you structure your next pitch (but arranged in no particular order):

1. **Be concise:** Get to the point! Aristotle's ancient but still great advice for any good speech:
   a. Tell them what you are going to tell them
   b. Tell them, and then
   c. Tell them what you told them.
2. **Start with your why:** A great way to connect with audiences is to start with why this film or project is important to you. Make an emotional connection as quickly as possible.
3. **Tease, but don't reveal:** Sometimes your audience will ask you to give away the ending, but your goal is to make them want more. Take them on a journey and create some tension in your pitch.
4. **What is your Why:** Why are you doing this project? Why are you the most qualified person to tell this story, and what is driving you to tell that story?

5. **Sum it up:** People forget most of the information you give them. After you pitch, sum it up and help them remember. At the end of your pitch, give a quick summary about the project.

6. **Create loglines:** As noted above, a logline is a one sentence description that sums up your film project in a concise, memorable and hopefully catchy way.

7. **Practice, practice, practice:** Know your project inside out. Practice in the mirror 100 times. Practice in front of people and get their feedback.

One of several pitches during the Black Public Media Bootcamp.

8. **Control the situation:** From the moment you get on stage or in front of a small group, you must visually and mentally own the space. Know your strengths and weaknesses and deal with them beforehand.

9. **Continuity equals power:** How you speak, your presence, and your actions must be consistent. When you are consistently in control, you will come off as very well prepared.

10. **Videotape your practice:** A great way to see how you look to people on stage is to record yourself, and then improve on things that you can improve upon. Are you fidgeting? Are you maintaining eye contact with your audience? Are you displaying

closed body language? Are you slurring your words or throwing in too much "verbal graffiti" (see below)?

11. **Get commitments from your audience:** Work on getting a call back and response. Get the audience engaged with your story, and ask them a question that gets them to respond in unison by nodding their heads in agreement. Get them to participate, raise their hands, laugh, etc. Psychologically get them to say "yes" by agreeing with you and your questions.

12. **Remove verbal graffiti:** Note how many "umms, "ughhhs," and "likes" have you used throughout your pitch. Count them, and then work on removing these from your pitch. Such verbal graffiti is distracting, and indicates that you do not know your material well enough.

13. **Lead with the genre:** Let the audience know right away the type of film you are creating. They may assume what the genre is, but you must make it clear to them right away so they aren't spending the rest of your pitch trying to figure out the genre while missing your entire pitch in the process.

14. **Strong delivery:** Remember, it's not so much what you say but how you say it that often influences people. Two people in the room could both have equally stunning projects, but the one who has the better delivery is the one who walks away with the check to fund the project.

15. **Make it memorable:** The easier your pitch is to remember and repeat, the more likely people are to re-pitch it to their colleagues.

16. **45 second rule:** Engage your audience in the first 45 seconds of your pitch.

17. **Avoid rambling:** Pace yourself. Pause. Silence helps create tension. There is nothing worse than a rambler. Rambling will make your short two-minute pitch feel like a torturous two-hour experience.

18. **First timers:** Every time you pitch, pitch as if everyone in the room is hearing it for the very first time even if they've heard it

20 times already. Don't assume that the audience knows all about you and the characters in your film.

19. **Do your research:** Know who you're pitching to. Pitching your horror film to a studio, film festival or executive that produces cartoons is just irresponsible. Also, research what previous projects the audience has funded. Companies want to replicate their success, so make sure that your project is a fit for them.

20. **Enthusiasm:** The energy of your pitch should match the energy of your project. If you are pitching a comedy, then your audience should be laughing during your pitch. If it's a thriller or drama, your pitch must be equally dramatic.

21. **Audience reaction:** Don't tell them how to feel, make them feel it. Think about how you want your audience to react, then move them in that direction with the story you tell.

22. **Equalize the transaction:** Make the buyer feel like they are gaining currency, not losing it.

23. **Sincerity:** Again, it's not about you. Think about them and what they need.

24. **Remove all doubt:** Plan ahead of time for some of the questions you might get during your pitch. Try to answer the audience's questions before they even have a chance to ask them. Here are a few major concerns an investor might have:
    a. Can I trust you?
    b. Does this person have my best interest in mind?
    c. What's in it for me?
    d. Do I need this right now?

25. **Create a sense of urgency:** There's nothing worse than the fear of missing out on something great. Create that tension! Make your audience feel like time is running out, and they need to act on this investment now!

26. **Find out what they're looking for:** This is more for a one-on-one meeting or with a smaller group of executives. Find out what's important to the executives by asking them to brag about their previous film successes. Use that information as leverage if

any of their previous shows targets the same audience that your project will reach.

27. **Make them feel good:** Any opportunity that you have to make the executives, audience or judges feel good about themselves will make them like you more, and put the odds in your favor because you made them feel good.

28. **Social proof:** If you've had a successful crowdfunding campaign or published works with a major brand, this is a way to build instant credibility with your audience. Nobody wants to be the first one at the party, but everyone wants to go to a party that's packed. The same goes for clients. Your projects suddenly have more appeal when everyone wants a piece of it.

29. **Visual aids:** Visual aids can help to prove the concepts that you are pitching. Make sure, however, that the production value is top quality, and not an obviously amateur effort because then those visual aids will hurt you. Also, don't lean too heavily on your visual aids. They are meant to supplement, not replace your pitch. In addition, make sure that you can easily handle or control your visual aids without fumbling or dropping them.

30. **Be a storyteller:** The most effective presenters are characters themselves. I'm not saying that you need to act like someone that you are not. Instead you should be as intriguing as your story. If you're not excited about your story, why should anyone else get excited?

BLACK PUBLIC MEDIA & PITCH BLACK AWARDS

Making a pitch to networks or a juried panel can be tough to do. I did it for the first time in April of 2019. I want to share a story with you about my first experience with pitching to a juried panel in front of a large audience full of executives from major networks.

In January 2019, I was accepted as a fellow into Black Public Media's 360 Incubator program. The incubator is a non-profit program in New York City designed to help support black filmmakers in developing their projects. The program also teaches filmmakers how to successfully pitch to major networks through a process similar to ABC's TV show "Shark Tank." *(Check them out at blackpublicmedia.org)*

BLACK PUBLIC MEDIA WEBSITE
Scan this QR Code to learn more about Black Public Media.

All of the fellows in the program were assigned a mentor who was an expert in the film industry. There were 13 contestants in three different categories. The winners of each category would receive between $50,000 and $150,000 towards the development of their projects along with intense, boot-camp styled training. The training included workshops on how to pitch, sustainability as a filmmaker, budgeting, marketing, and much more. This experience definitely took me out of my comfort zone while teaching me the importance of believing in myself. With so many distractions around me, my biggest fear was that I would allow myself to lose focus. I had to isolate myself as much as possible which was hard to do with three children screaming to get my attention at home.

FILMMAKERS BOOT CAMP

During the two-week boot camp training program, we were visited by a new guest speaker each day. Since they knew nothing about us, we would have to go around the room and explain who we were and what our projects would be. The guest speakers would then randomly ask for volunteers to come up to pitch their films with no preparation, no rehearsal - just come up and pitch!

Taking notes alongside fellow filmmakers during the bootcamp.

Well, it's not hard to imagine that no one raised their hands. As I looked around the room, however, I always put my hand up and volunteered to go first. Everyone thought that I was pretty brave for doing that. In fact, one of the directors would later comment to my assigned mentor, Kimson Albert, in a phone conversation that I was "fearless."

Boy, did I fool them - I was terrified! However, I wanted to convince myself that I was ready for this, so I purposely and consistently threw myself into the line of fire. In the process, I ended up changing people's perceptions of me. Most importantly, it changed the perceptions that I had of myself.

Whether you chose to take the lead or just sit back and do nothing, you are building a reputation for yourself. Throughout the two weeks of boot camp, we had great guest speakers and several impromptu pitch sessions. With each new guest speaker, there was that little fear that they might ask us to randomly come up and give a pitch. We filmmakers were constantly put on the spot in a series of nerve-racking practice pitches and exercises. As brutal as the process seemed at that moment, I realize now that they were just trying to break us out of our comfort zones.

On the seventh day of boot camp, we had our third practice pitch session, and I was slated to go up first. I got dressed up in shirt and tie and stayed up all night rehearsing. When I went up to make my pitch, I absolutely bombed! It was a disaster.

My "sins": I exceeded my 10 minutes, didn't finish my pitch, wasn't sure of my material, didn't connect with the audience, and was uptight and uncomfortable. This was a rare negative performance for me. I took all the feedback I got, and used it to help strengthen my pitch methods. After the boot camp ended, I spent over two months working on strengthening my pitch material.

We were told to practice our pitches so that we would be ready when we returned to New York City several months later. Upon our return, we had to endure four days of around-the-clock practice pitches before the big pitch day a few days later. Remembering what worked and didn't work from my previous pitches, I went up dressed down. I was super relaxed. I went off script, added a quiz, and gave away prizes.

PRACTICE PITCH VIDEO

Scan this QR Code to view a clip of one of my practice pitches.

Those changes turned my pitch into an entertaining conversation. My attitude about the pitch had changed and, as a result, my performance improved. I was actually having fun with it now, and was confident of my pitch. The thing that really helped me the most was my ability to go off script. Every single time an opportunity came up to speak in front of an audience, I jumped at it. Scared or not, I took it. In facing my fear of pitching a product I wasn't sure about yet, I got over my fears which helped me focus on my delivery, my body language, and my engagement with the audience. My consistent behavior became my norm. Everyone expected nothing less from me from that point on, including me! Your actions, good or bad, will begin to shape people's perception of you.

PITCH NIGHT

It was Pitch Day. All of the practicing, all of the pitches in front of a mirror, all of the feedback and advice had led up to this moment. I had a lot riding on this as I had traveled to New York City with my three kids, and I did not want to let them down. Each finalist had to convince the judges and audience members that our individual projects were worthy of financial support.

It was only a 10-minute pitch. Even though I had a script rehearsed, I knew early on that the most successful practice pitches I had done were the mostly unscripted pitches. This was the tactic that I would use on Pitch Night. While I thought the pitch was well received, I had no idea if it would prove to be a winner.

PITCH NIGHT VIDEO
Scan this QR Code to view the 10-minute pitch and 10-minute Q&A video clip.

AWARD CEREMONY

On April 12, 2019, the award ceremony had arrived. I had come to the conclusion that regardless of the outcome, I had already won. I was so proud of myself for stepping out of my comfort zone to propel the trajectory of my brand.

My brother Edwin and his wife joined me at the ceremony while my mother and three kids waited anxiously at home. I had riveting conversations with several people at the dinner table that night. Once the names were called in my category and I heard my name announced as the winner, the rest of the night was a blur.

I had not prepared an acceptance speech, but to stay consistent with all of my previous jovial pitch sessions, I opened with a silly joke (which was well received by the audience). This entire process helped strengthen my confidence in myself and in my abilities as not just an artist, but as an influencer. At the end of the day, your artwork will outlive you. What message do you want people to take away after they see your work?

ACCEPTANCE SPEECH VIDEO

Scan this QR Code to view my acceptance speech at the award ceremony.

A final thought: I often remind myself, though, not to mistake motion with progress. You can be very busy moving around occupying your time doing freelance projects for tons of clients, but how much of it makes a real impact? I have become devoted to ensuring the work that I take on has a purpose. You, too, should think about that as it can be a real motivator to everything you do.

Chapter Eleven

SETTING AND ACCOMPLISHING GOALS

THE BENEFITS OF FREELANCING WHILE HOLDING A 9-5 JOB

It's no secret: millions of people across the world are working jobs that they hate. For several years, I hated my job, too. Even though you would rather dive head first into a pool of molten lava than to have to go back to work tomorrow, there are some benefits to launching your freelance career while holding down a fulltime job.

A key benefit is that you have a steady income stream to allow you to flexibly test your products and services in the marketplace. Small businesses often lack working capital. When you have a guaranteed paycheck coming in, that gives you more breathing room to explore new ideas with your own business. Here are a few other quick benefits to keep in mind:

- **Steady Paycheck:** Use your steady paycheck to fund some of your freelance projects. Having a steady paycheck makes you a stronger negotiator. If you blow a deal with a client, it's okay - you still have another paycheck coming in. Use that moment to sharpen your negotiation skills.

- **Job Resources:** What resources does your job make available to you such as discounts on supplies, merchandise, or possibly even airline tickets? Use whatever resources your current job might have available to you as employee. A cautionary note here: don't be "borrowing" resources (some might use the "steal" word) to benefit your freelance business!

- **Health Benefits:** One of the major benefits of keeping your full-time job while you freelance are health benefits. While the Freelancers Union (freelancersunion.org) and the Affordable Care Act (healthcare.gov) are just two places you can apply for healthcare plans if you're self-employed, such insurance isn't cheap. Don't jump from your "bird's nest" prematurely - be intentional. Budget your money and account for potentially expensive monthly insurance premiums once you go out on your own.

- **Peace of mind:** While you can't necessarily put a dollar amount on peace of mind, there is no doubt that the knowledge of a steady income puts your mind at ease. Take some of your bigger risks while you have gainful employment. You can recoup your freelance financial losses quicker when you have a job.

- **Learn on the job:** Some of the best self-employed entrepreneurs are good company employees. Be the first one in and the last one out at the company that you work for. Learn as much as you can about your job. Are there any experts in your company that may be willing to mentor you or give you their expert advice on business generally? Investing in yourself is the best stock there is.

PLEASE DON'T QUIT YOUR DAY JOB (AT LEAST NOT YET!)

In 2002, I landed my dream job at the Walt Disney Feature Animation company in Burbank, California. However, it seemed that growth opportunities were available to everyone except me. Four years later, I was still in the same position. I applied to every single position posted on the internal job boards. My ultimate goal at the time was to make it as an Animation Director and grow within the company but I was always overlooked. It was such a great company to work for, and I worked with some of the most amazing and incredibly talented people in the country. Still, I felt trapped.

I was getting restless. Certainly, I did not want to stick around, and wait to see how long it would take before my skills would be recognized on the job. I realized then that the plans that I had for myself were bigger than those my current employer had for me. The more I thought about it, the angrier I got. Then I moved from anger to hate, and with that, I began complaining about everything and looked for new reasons to hate my job even more.

If someone sneezed the wrong way, I got upset. If the free Disneyland tickets that were given to employees twice a year had Mickey Mouse on them instead of Donald Duck, I got upset. (Clearly everyone knew just how much I preferred Donald Duck over Mickey Mouse!)

I came to the conclusion that if I worked for myself, everything would be alright. So, without a plan, without carefully assessing the pros and cons of self-employment, choosing to purposely ignore the heartfelt advice of all of my dear family, friends, co-workers and mentors; I made an emotional decision and gave my two weeks' notice. I mean, come on, how could this decision possibly blow up in my face? The answer to that question came a lot sooner than I expected.

THE STARVING ARTIST

Quitting your stable full-time job without a plan to start an unstable freelance business with no prior business experience is very much like jumping into the freezing cold, shark infested ocean without a life jacket! You may not see the danger right away, but rest assured trouble is right around the corner. Well, when I quit my job, I didn't just jump into the shark infested waters. Instead I was holding two 20-pound sacks full of bloody steaks under each arm. The sharks of life were about to rip me to shreds.

Looking back now, I don't regret leaving the company but I will admit this: it would have made more sense for me to have set some goals, developed a plan, and gotten some mentors to guide me on how to generate new revenue streams instead of abruptly leaving the company. The first month after leaving went well. I sold new merchandise, and had some of my new products featured on one of the top Latin websites in the country which resulted in major sales that month. I was on top of the world! But it wouldn't last. Weeks later, no matter how hard I tried, I wasn't able to make a single sale.

This shouldn't have come as a big surprise though. I didn't have a business plan, a marketing strategy, a business coach, or enough money saved up to get me through the next six months. As much as I hated to admit it, just three months after quitting my day job, I had officially become a "starving artist."

A TOTAL LOSS

Six months after quitting, I swallowed my pride and started applying for full-time work. I landed a job at State Farm Insurance Company. Ironically, I worked in the "total loss" department that only handled cases where vehicles were totally wrecked beyond repair. What a coincidence since I was feeling like a total loss with an art career that was now wrecked beyond repair.

I often found myself drawing motivational sketches and pinning them to my new cubicle wall in the hopes of lifting my spirits. Soon, I had dozens of little drawings all around my cubicle. I didn't know it at the time, but this was a clear violation of company policy. Any employee who had three major infractions had grounds for being fired.

After only one month into the job, I already had two infractions against me: one for the cubicle drawings and the other for spending 60 minutes at a company-wide meeting drawing people instead of taking notes.

The State Farm designs that got me into trouble.

154

Needless to say, I felt like I was walking on eggshells. If I laughed too loud, or sneezed in the wrong direction, I feared that I would get written up. A little poetic justice, I guess. It was a rough time in my life, and I felt defeated. Just when I thought things couldn't get any worse, I made another emotional decision (no, I still hadn't learned my lesson: I decided to give up art entirely. I was so full of self-doubt that I willingly buried my passion for drawing in that building.

WHAT ARE YOU DOING HERE?

At this point, I never thought that I would ever get out of the mental jail cell that I created for myself. It took a supervisor who I didn't know to get me back on the track. One day, while I was sulking at my cubicle, a supervisor named Gary walked by and asked me to join him in his office. Oh, no - another infraction?

I followed him into his office and he closed the door. He stared at me for a few seconds before either of us said a word. He opened by stating how much he loved his job. "I love insurance and I am very good at what I do," he said. "I get up in the morning and it's the first thing I think about. My purpose is to help people feel secure in their time of ultimate distress and vulnerability." He paused, walked over to me and looked me in the eyes and asked, "What are you doing here?"

I thought it was a rhetorical question so I stayed quiet. He went on to say, "I work here because I am positively impacting lives every day. I don't know you, but I know enough to know that you don't belong here. Don't you see, the cause of all of your trouble in this company is the one thing that you are most passionate about, your art? You belong in an environment that will allow you to express your creativity. If none exists, create your own. Write out a plan and then put it into action. Don't sit around waiting for something to happen, go out and make it happen."

I've heard it said before - good things do not come to those who wait, they come to those who hustle. I teared up, gave him a hug, walked over to my desk, and began writing out my goals for the next three years of my life. Once I completed all that, I folded up the paper, removed my badge, left my work keys in the drawer, walked out of the building and never looked back.

One week after leaving the insurance company, I landed a job as a character animator for an independent animation studio. The nightmare was finally over. While technically I did just "quit another day job," the difference this time was that I had a plan, I set some goals and set out to accomplish them. I then surrounded myself with mentors, and started reading books on business. When your attitude changes, so too will the trajectory of your career.

MANAGING YOUR FINANCES

Managing your finances is not an easy task. It gets even more difficult when you have sporadic revenue streams coming in. You can't plan for income that you don't know you're going to get. Worse yet, some projects will involve delayed payments or clients will set their payroll system to pay you in 30-90 days. The feeling of always being strapped for cash is a constant one. Don't back yourself into a corner - be prepared for the storm!

Here are a few things that you can do to help you manage your finances and improve your economic growth.

- **Diversify income streams:** Don't put your eggs in one basket. I know, it's cliché, but it's so true. If the source of your revenue is solely from one client, you're going to be in trouble when the client announces the end of the project. It has happened to me and trust me - it's never a good feeling having the rug pulled out from beneath you.
- **Emergency fund:** The unpredictability of freelancing can be tough to deal with. One month you might be going out for lobster dinners, and another month you'll be salivating over that peanut butter and jelly sandwich because it's all you can afford. An emergency fund will help you get by when your business account is getting low. Ideally, you want to have enough money in your account to cover expenses for six months.

- **Avoid extra banking fees:** I once paid $36 for a water bottle. Why? At the time of I purchased the $1 water bottle, my bank account was in the red with a negative balance. I ended up paying $35 overdraft fee due to insufficient funds. With online banking these days, you should be able to avoid such overdraft fees.

- **Give yourself a paycheck:** When you land a client, deposit the check into your savings account. Then, set an amount to be transferred to your checking account every two weeks or once a month. The idea is that this is the paycheck you will use to cover your expenses for the month. Ration your funds and only use what is in your checking account. Make sure that your debit card is not linked to your savings account so that you're not tempted to just start dipping into your savings account.

- **Set money aside for taxes:** You should talk to your tax preparer for an accurate amount of money you should be setting aside. It will vary depending on the type of products and services you offer. In some situations, you may need to pay estimated tax.

- **Track your expenses:** Check your bank account as often as you check your social media pages. What are your spending habits? Is there anything that you can cut? That $5 coffee is much cheaper (and will last longer) if you buy a bag and brew it yourself at home. By browsing your spending history, you will be able to pinpoint needless expenditures and reduce your monthly expenses. Spend your money wisely. Be sure, too, that you save every receipt reflecting expenses that you have had to pay for your freelance business. You'll need those receipts when tax preparation time rolls around.

- **Set milestones & collect deposits:** Hands down, the biggest financial struggle is rarely being able to dictate when you will receive payment from your clients. Always get a deposit to start any project and then set payment milestones. After you complete a specific phase (milestone) in the project, you will be able to request another payment. This way, at least, you set up a payment schedule for yourself along with a little assurance that, in the next couple of weeks, you will have some money to work with as long as you deliver your work on time.

CONSISTENTLY CRUSH YOUR GOALS

You can accomplish any attainable goal that you set for your business. It starts with changing your vocabulary from "I will try and get this done today," into "I will start this task right now." Notice how you speak to yourself. Make a conscious effort to stop saying **"I can't."**

The greatest plan in the world means nothing if you don't take action on it. Just get started! Here are some tips to help you consistently crush your goals!

- **Prepare the night before:** When you set your goals for the day, get into the habit of writing them down the night before your day actually starts. This way, when you start your day, you're getting right to business and not wasting anytime. Your freelance business will not get ahead if you're not constantly thinking ahead.

- **Time Management:** Growing a freelance business while you have a full-time job can be a real challenge. Carve out some time every night to invest in your business. If you work 9-5, then take from 6-10 to work on your dream. If you can't find the time, make the time! Otherwise you freelance business will just be a dream.

- **Expect the unexpected:** Freelancing is unpredictable, but the one thing that you can predict is that things will not always go as planned. When you anticipate problems, you will be better equipped to turn these obstacles into opportunities. The thing about setting goals is that they should be things that you really want to accomplish. This way when unexpected obstacles arrive, the hardships won't be enough to stop you. It's just another bump in the road.

- **Write 'em down and put 'em up:** Buy yourself a large dry erase board and write down your daily goals for the day. Hang the whiteboard up in a place that you will see several times a day. It becomes easier to envision your goals when you see them written down. To take it a step further, write the goals on your phone and set alerts, add pop ups on your laptop, and scribble those goals on Post It notes. Write your goals down in multiple places and immerse yourself in what you want to accomplish.

- **Revert back to Monotasking:** If you look up the word "multi-task" in the English dictionary, you would probably see a picture of a freelancer. However, studies have shown that focusing all of your efforts on one task at a time is much more productive than attempting to handle multiple tasks. Prioritize your most number one important task for the day and crush it.

- **Reward yourself:** Incentives are great motivators. As a self-employed freelancer, you might not have someone to pat you on the back every time you accomplish a new goal. I encourage you to celebrate your own successes. Knocked out all your goals for the day, week or month? Treat yourself to something nice! You deserve it.

- **Set deadlines:** Hold yourself accountable. Look at your calendar and block in dates that you would like to complete your goals by. Set daily, weekly and monthly deadlines for yourself. You will become much more efficient with your time when you know you only have a few days left to complete a specific project.

- **Keep it simple:** Know your limitations so that you don't bite off more than you can chew. It's easy to start a to-do list and, by the time you're done writing it, you need two sheets of paper to complete it. Keep it simple by setting one to two major goals for the day. If you routinely crush your goals, focus on two major goals for the day. It's all about quality, not quantity.

- **Be specific:** Clearly outline what you want to accomplish so that you can come up with plans of attack. Put some thought into your daily goals and how they contribute to your long-term goal. Be specific, and modify those goals as your situation changes.

- **Be realistic:** Set goals that are attainable. Surround yourself with people who have accomplished some of the things you want to accomplish. Use them as inspiration. If you can't find anyone in person, find them on the shelves in a bookstore.

- **It should excite you:** The goals that you set should have you waking up excited to get started. Think about the impact that crushing this goal will make in your personal or professional life. No matter how small the daily goal is, it should keep you motivated.

- **Track your growth:** How are you measuring the growth of your business? Is it based on income, the size of your network, or perhaps the impact that you have made on others throughout the year? Whatever your benchmark is, you want to be sure that you can track your progress. You want to be able to crush your goals! Don't, however, create an unrealistic list of goals that will crush you. Ask yourself if what you're doing today is getting you closer to where you want to be tomorrow.

FINAL THOUGHTS

Whatever goals you are looking to accomplish for yourself or your freelance business, plan for it, and go out and get it. Keep in mind that you want to obtain laser-like focus, but you don't want tunnel vision either. Check out what's going on around you, read books, do research, but never compromise your voice. Your authenticity is what will always set you apart from everyone else.

I did not start accomplishing my business objectives until I started believing that I could. You won't win all the time and that's okay. I have been rejected more times than I care to count. Clients have told me "no" more than they have said yes. I have negotiated really bad deals, and have spent hours putting together proposals that clients never even opened.

In short (to reference an old baseball movie), I have built "it" and they did not come. Despite my overwhelming losses, I never stopped trying. Success comes when you work towards turning your proverbial lemons into lemonade. Learn from your mistakes and move on.

Often times when working in my office, sitting alone, I had to find ways to combat the isolation. I started taking lunch breaks outside. I would bring lunch to work, but I just chose to eat it in a public place. Your obstacles may be different, but know that there is always a possible solution.

After reading this book, I hope that you now feel empowered and energized to get into the freelancing business. I hope that you are inspired to invest in yourself. Whatever side hustles or businesses you were thinking of trying, that you are now motivated to put a plan together and start it! This is the only life you will get to make it happen. If you try and it doesn't work, learn from that and try again. You have to keep challenging yourself and stepping out of your comfort zone in order to grow. I would prefer that you set a goal that is "super high," and land somewhere in the middle instead of setting a "super low" goal and hitting it.

Do you really want to spend the rest of your life sulking or complaining about that job that you wish you had? As Gary from the insurance company told me, if the opportunity does not exist, create one. Sabotaging your success and giving up on your dreams because of a temporary circumstance that you may find yourself in at the time will clearly get you nowhere.

Remember this, too: the plans that you have for yourself will always be greater than those others have for you. There are resources available to support you. Get a mentor or get a business coach from the Small Business Development Center. You don't have to tackle it all on your own!

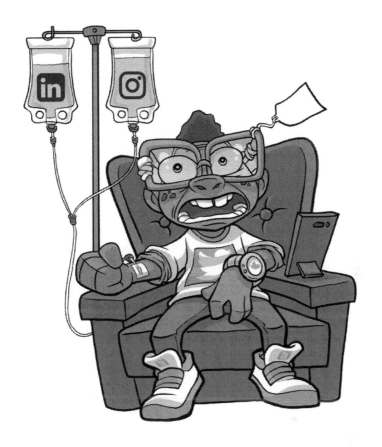

Scan the QR Codes of your choice
and let's connect online today!

INSTAGRAM

LINKEDIN

FACEBOOK